Bridges to Heaven

True Stories of Loved Ones on the Other Side

Sue Frederick

Also by Sue Frederick

I See Your Soul Mate
I See Your Dream Job

Bridges to Heaven

True Stories of Loved Ones on the Other Side

Sue Frederick

#

Library of Congress Cataloging-in-Publication Data (**TK**)

ISBN 978-0-9762393-5-2
EAN 978-1-250-00181-8

First U.S. Edition: September 2013

10 9 8 7 6 5 4 3 2 1

Dedication

To Paul and Crissie whose early deaths brought me to my knees in despair – and then kept me there in awe.

Acknowledgments

Sending a big hug of gratitude to all of you beautiful souls who've shared your deepest pain and your extraordinary gifts in our sessions, workshops, classes, webinars and friendships. Your brave stories inspire me everyday and are the reason I do this work. I feel divinely blessed by your company and love meeting you wherever I go.

Thank you to every one of you, especially those who allowed me to share your stories in this book and have helped me in numerous other wonderful ways: Kim Shannon, Katherine Dreyer, Kat Garrard, Pam Porter, Linda Long, Isabella Cappucci, Joan Frederick, Judy Colburn, Wanda Morrison, Debi Brown, Charlene Ellington, Lisa Livingstone, Deb Davis, Dolores Rollins, Cindy Covington, Sharon Reese, Gwen Barbee, Donna Davis, Marty Traynor, Barbara Wainwright, Berry Fowler, Erin Tillotsen and many others that I can't possibly name here.

Big huge hugs and kisses to my editor Jennifer Enderlin and my agent Lisa Hagan. I'm forever grateful to you both!

My deepest gratitude goes to my husband and soul mate Gene and our two magnificent children – Sarah and Kai.

As always I offer abundant love and prayer to my posse of divine guides including Nityananda and the many departed loved ones (Paul, Crissie, Marv, dad, Uncle Pete and on) who continue to guide and help me get this work right.

Most importantly, thank you God for helping me find my way through this dense energy realm where I've gotten lost more than once and have often forgotten that I came here on purpose to fulfill my soul's mission.

Your love and light has always lifted the veil in my hour of need, revealing the divine realms, reminding me that I'm a soul on a brief journey, and showing me clearly where to take my next step. I devote everything to you.

Contents

Preface

Grief pushes you into the deep ocean of your soul's wisdom; it breaks your heart wide open.

In a Dream ...
I'm standing on a beach, surrounded by a vast expanse of dark sand as far as I can see. Gulls are squawking in the distance. I'm looking into my father's watery blue eyes. He's animated and young, explaining something to me with more passion than I ever saw in the last years of his life. His brother, my beloved uncle Pete, who died soon after my dad, is standing beside us, laughing.

We're enjoying the vivid openness of the sand and sky and sharing stories, when behind them in the distance, I see a huge tidal wave rolling along the sand toward us—maybe a hundred feet high and towering ominously over the flat landscape. We turn and see another powerful wave rolling directly toward us from the opposite direction. We're standing between these two oncoming waves, and in an instant, we realize there's nothing we can do.

I grab their hands. "How will we remember?" I ask, staring into their eyes. "How will we find each other again?"

"Don't worry," answers my uncle Pete. "We always find each other."

He shouts something else, but I can't hear his words through the sound of the crashing waves. I wake up gasping for breath—still feeling their strong hands wrapped around mine— longing for that moment again, hearing their voices in my head, unable to get back to sleep.

Do we always find each other again? Isn't that endless longing the tyranny of grief? Or is it simply our limited perspective on time and space? Aren't we longing for the divine realms, where everything and everyone is luminous and connected—and aching to return to a home we can't quite remember?

When our loved ones step into the other realms, they never fully leave us. We abandon them—by not believing they're still with us. We stop listening. Our pain blocks them out.

Of course, we're angry that our loved ones left us alone when we needed them. And we're angry with the doctor who didn't diagnose the cancer or the drunk driver on the road that night. But mostly, we're angry with ourselves because we might have prevented it if only we had . . .

Yes, there's plenty to be angry about in the physical world, and life is unfair—until you realize it's all on purpose. This tragic event is only a brief blip in your soul's journey. Grief is in your life today to help you. It's your divine reveal—pushing you to remember who you really are and what you came to do.

There's no teacher as powerful as Divine Mother Grief—the spiritual master of pain and enlightenment. If you've chosen Mother Grief as your teacher, you're clearly a powerful old soul who came here to do great work and to help raise the consciousness of humanity. You're here to be a beacon of light for others. And yes, of course you'll make your living from these gifts and find the love you crave. It's all waiting for you to take a step in a new direction.

Let me take you on a journey to the divine. I'll unfold your wings and help you remember how to fly. We'll soar into the vast ocean of the higher realms. We'll leave your pain behind.

Then you'll remember that you came from a world of grace and light and will return to it soon enough—and that this earth-bound life is your brief dream. You'll see your departed ones dancing in the ethers and soaring through your house like children at play.

This part here—this physical world—is the hard part. But you came here on purpose to educate yourself, expand your boundaries, and emerge brilliant and powerful. You're not a victim—no matter how tragic your story.

When you're stuck in your grief, your departed loved one sees you wrapped in a gray cloud of negative energy and longs to take away your pain. Your grief keeps your loved ones from communicating with you. It becomes a wall they can't break through.

Those wasted days of feeling not good enough, strong enough, smart enough, or saying, "I don't care," are when we disappoint our higher selves and push away our departed.

When you once again open your heart and trust your intuition, you'll hear your departed speaking. You'll embrace your spirituality and help others. You'll walk away from the bitterness that damages your soul and separates you from love.

Mother Grief will teach you ultimately that your life must have meaning and purpose or there's no reason to be here, and only you hold the key to finding that purpose. This book reveals your soul's mission and illuminates your next steps. But you have to take the first step. . . .

If you seek only to stop the pain, your pain increases exponentially. Addictions and distractions pull you off course and make your journey harder. When you trust your higher self instead, you become a beacon of light for the world. And that is why you came here.

This painful moment is your spiritual reawakening—provided courtesy of your higher self. It's your moment of grace. There's only one solution now—fulfill your soul's mission and become the light being you came here to be. Here and now, you get to choose. Everything you need is here. All is forgiven. And you— you are divine. And this is your moment.

Introduction: When Your Loved One Dies

If you're grieving today, know that your departed tries to ease your pain. Be still and listen. . . .

I'm standing in front of an audience of two hundred or more people—teaching a weekend workshop to help them see their true work, their souls' mission. A woman raises her hand, and I catch a brief glimpse of a man standing beside her, wearing a baseball cap pulled down low over his eyes. She tells me her husband died recently and left her very little money. She left the workforce twenty years ago—to raise their three kids and help her husband manage the paperwork for his business. Now she's lost without her husband and her husband's income. Can I help her?

As she tells me her sad story, I see that her spirit is luminous and glowing. I quickly calculate her birth path and see that she's a master soul on the path of the sacred number 11— here to inspire and heal others. She has great work yet to do. I see her counseling people and teaching workshops in the future. Clearly, this grief she's experiencing is meant to fuel her reinvention.

The man beside her nods and sends me the message: "She's got more gifts than I ever had. It's time for her to believe in herself. Tell her to be a therapist. It's why she's still there. It's her turn. There's money for her."

I tell her this information and explain that this work is her soul's mission and she'll be great at it. She says it's funny because she has dreamt of going back to school to study psychology—the only thing she's really interested in. But how could she afford it? The man nods again. "The money is there," he says.

When I give her this message, she argues that there's no money. She repeats her sad story, and I can tell she's not ready to let the story go or give it a new ending. I move on and continue teaching the workshop, often aware of the presence of the man with the baseball cap. During a break, I close my eyes and speak directly to him: "She needs your guidance to find a way to finance school. Where is the money? You have to tell her."

At the end of the two-day workshop, the woman approaches me. "I had a dream last night," she says. "My husband told me there was another insurance policy. He was always so disorganized—putting papers everywhere. But now I think I know where I'll find it when I'm home. I may be able to go back to school after all. We'll see." She's smiling radiantly as she tells me this. It's the beginning of her new story.

Another day while preparing to work with a client, I see two lovely gentlemen sitting in front of me during my meditation. "Tell her she's the gifted one, not us," they say, chuckling with each other. "Tell her she has the gift of storytelling and must use it. She can write and tell her own story in a documentary. She's so beautiful and talented, but she doesn't see her own gifts," says the older one.

I call my client and begin the session, sharing my vision. She's spent years promoting the work of her husband and his brother— both successful artists and both departed. Clearly, they want her to focus on her own gifts now. She's a writer and it's time for her own story to be told. After our session, it takes a while for her to change directions, release the focus on her departed loved ones and their gifts, and refocus on her own path. But eventually she does, and her great work unfolds beautifully.

Hours of conversations with spirits and sharing those conversations with clients have shown me beyond any doubt that our departed loved ones try hard to get us to listen to them. They try repeatedly to help us see a bigger vision of who we are and what we're here to do—even if this isn't how they behaved while they were here. Crossing over changes everything. . . .

A woman looking very tired approaches me in the long line to get her book signed. Her girlfriend is at her side—with her arm wrapped tightly around the exhausted woman's waist. The girlfriend tells me that this woman just lost her young son to cancer. She's not doing well, says the friend. "Can you see her child's spirit?" she asks.

Yes, I sense him. He's a bright, dancing sprite beside her, silly and giggling— pulling on her arm. But she's defeated and heavy of heart and can't feel it. I sense she may have a drug numbing her, a drug given by a kind doctor meaning to help. But the drug (probably prescribed for depression) prevents her from feeling her beautiful boy dancing beside her; instead, she feels only a light breeze against her skin and dismisses it.

How can I help her see him? I tell her that he's fine and happy and dances beside her and wants her to be happy. I ask her to close her eyes with me for a moment and feel his energy. We hold hands in silence. I can feel her son's energy acting up— jumping around us. He says, "Mom, I'm here. I'm fine." She smiles at me briefly and there are tears in her eyes. "I think I can feel him," she says. "But I've never believed in an afterlife "

I explain that this grief is her moment of spiritual reawakening. I tell her to sit in quiet meditation every morning and ask to feel her child's presence. I tell her to speak to him directly during her meditation and write down any thoughts or images that come to her. If she does this, I explain, it will bring her own spirit back to life. She'll know beyond any doubt that her boy is happy and well. She tells me she'll do it.

Because of her heavy heart, I pray she'll make the effort. A huge part of her doesn't really believe her little boy lives on—even as he tugs at her sleeve. She has spent most of her life dismissing her higher self and intuition, and being cynical. She's in a deep spiritual crisis now. Her departed son is fine—shining in the light like a little Buddha beside her—wanting so desperately for Mom to feel better. But Mom must do the work of reawakening to her higher self.

It's *her* soul that's sleeping, not her little boy's. It's time for her to remember who she is and why she's here. Her son's departure is meant to inspire this spiritual reawakening. This is the soul mate agreement she made with him long before this lifetime began. As she languishes in pain, she misses the point, misunderstands the agreement, and makes her journey more difficult.

I tell her to e-mail me about her progress. A year later, I hear from her. She says that after months of languishing in grief, she began to meditate. She tells me it has been miraculous—that she *can* hear her son's voice when she sits and quiets her mind. And this experience, she says, has launched her life in a new and hopeful direction.

We are the ones who die when we grieve our loved ones. The departed pray for our pain to go away, for us to realize that it's all on purpose, and that we can join them as soon as we fulfill our mission here, and help ease the pain of others.

The voices of my departed are an endless song in my head. They move my hands across the keyboard and fill my nights with dreams. I'm their child left behind whom they watch with great concern and extraordinary love—holding back when they long to help, staying quiet when I take a wrong turn, letting me learn my lessons as a child learns to walk by falling down and getting back up again.

From the moment I met Paul under the white-hot streetlight, silver halo wrapped around his head, eyes ripped from a vivid ocean blue sky—I knew I belonged with him. How gracefully he saw me, stroking my hair to find perfection in every flaw, seeing beauty in every crease. He laid his hands upon my soul and loved me.

We shared such joy in our escapades: the long hikes to climb ridiculous peaks, the God talks, the movies that made us laugh and cry.

With his dreams wrapped inside my heart, I saw our future unfold. This love would be a resting place for me— somewhere I felt safe from a world where my gifts pushed me too far to the left of normal. I needed his arms around me to dig in— to create our white picket fence life. Together we would find a way to make this realm our own, do our good work and thrive. He made me happy every day.

Did I know he would die soon? I'm intuitive. Why didn't I see it?

It came to me in so many ways so that I would be prepared. Yet being the hardheaded child I was, I fought against each divine reveal: the look on the technician's face the day they scanned Paul's liver, how that film was lost and never found again, the misdiagnosis that made no sense. On our first hospital stay, a man Paul's age, dying of end-stage colon cancer, was wheeled in to be our roommate. While Paul was still learning what it meant to have a tumor in his intestines, this dying young man and his desperate wife (named Sue) gave us a glimpse into a future we didn't want to see. We quickly asked to be moved to a different room.

And what if I *had* heeded the signs, would it have helped? I'm sure I could have been more graceful. I could have moved our bed down from the upstairs bedroom sooner. I didn't need to throw my glass of iced tea against the wall the night the canister leaked bile all over the sheets. So dramatic. But my perfect future was slowly and painfully being ripped from my hands. Our white picket fence was crumbling.

Did Paul know where the journey would take us? How it would end up here with me speaking to you? He spoke in riddles at the end, telling me I was gifted, demanding that I not waste my life grieving for him. He made impossible demands on my heart.

I must have been the baby soul of our posse—struggling to keep up with those I loved. When they asked for a volunteer to drop into the physical realms and accomplish something hard, to be strong and help raise the limits of consciousness, I must have raised my hand—not really knowing what it entailed. But knowing I had to do something big and vast and brave—or be left behind. I remember someone telling me I had a courageous heart; it was just a whisper and then I was gone. How many hours have been wasted here in my pity? It's hard to tell. But all that matters is before I leave this lifetime, before it's done, *you* have heard me.

Part 1

Lifting the Thin Veil
Between the Realms

Chapter One

STORIES OF VISITATION

The veil between the realms is thinner than you think—thin and transparent. Close your eyes and feel it. . . .

There was never a time when spirits didn't speak to me, walk across my bedroom at night, or whisper in my ear. They speak to you as well. You're just better able to dismiss it, more logically rooted in this physical world than I am—even though I've tried hard to ground myself in logical left-brain thinking.

Somewhere in my 1951 birthing, there was probably a vast undiscovered damage to my perfect brain—so big and precise, it nearly diminished my left mind and left me mostly connected to the heavenly realms.

From early on, there were radiant beings who spoke to me in the flower garden where my mother planted daisies—and departed saints who stood beside me every Sunday in church. It's a blessing I was Catholic; the Virgin Mary was a constant presence in my life, one so real that I spoke to her out loud. I prayed the rosary daily from the time I learned how.

The mysterious city of New Orleans made my gifts seem almost normal. My intuitive Creole mother, descended from a long line of psychic women, was strong enough to see what I needed and help me get firmly rooted here. She spent her afternoons teaching me letters, sounding out the words precisely and logically until I could develop my left brain and read the pages. I was only three years old. It saved me. She believed I was gifted.

When I grew older and would hear what someone was going to say before they said it, time fell backwards and I withdrew. I'm sure I looked disturbed, troubled. I didn't understand the laughter and why they couldn't hear the whispers of those who stood around us. But I didn't like crazy. I was way too strong for that.

So I hit the dirt. Sprang into survival mode. I learned to think logically—to follow from A to B, to ignore the visions and dreams. I didn't want to disappoint my kind and logical father. I needed a paycheck. And when the whispers began to fade, I found myself an early career at the age of twenty, teaching children to read and organize their left brains because that was what I needed. I became a Montessori preschool teacher to heal myself.

If I'd only known all along I was here to explain the world as I saw it—and not try to fit in or become like everyone else—I could have gotten my work done sooner. I've taken quite a while to get this message to you, to help you realize the veil is thin, and that you came here on purpose with a mission. Yet this is the one thing I've always been sure of, and the gift I came to share.

My Father . . .

It's May 1997. My dad, diagnosed with lung cancer four weeks earlier, has been in a coma for days, struggling for breath. My family takes turns caring for him at the hospital. I want to stay at his side today because I sense he's leaving. Yet it's my turn to babysit his five grandchildren—including my three-year-old daughter.

I kiss my dad on the forehead, tell him I love him and will see him soon. Back at Grandmother's house, I put the kids down to nap. Finally, they sleep. I'm free to meditate, as I've done every day for thirty years.

Sitting on the couch, I close my eyes and repeat a mantra—an ancient Sanskrit sacred sound. Right away, my mind settles down. Instantly, my father is vividly in front of me, laughing and being goofy. He's young and healthy. I'm delighted to see him happy and animated. This image is so real and tangible that I smile and say playfully, "Dad, what are you doing here?"

"Dad!" I repeat out loud, opening my eyes—realizing that I've just clearly seen my dad who's in a hospital miles away—dying. I pick up the phone to call the hospital room. My brother answers.

"Jim, what's happening? I just saw Dad."

"He's had a heart attack. We're trying to stop the CPR efforts. It's chaos."

"I was meditating and he appeared in front of me—alive and happy."

"That's amazing, Sue. You're psychic," he says sweetly but sarcastically. "Now, put the kids back in the car and come down here."

By the time I reach the hospital with my entourage of cranky toddlers, Dad's body is laid out peacefully on the hospital bed and my family is gathered around, crying. I'm upset that I wasn't with him.

"He's gone," Jim says as I enter. "But you were with him more than we were. It was chaos here when it happened. You saw him as soon as he crossed over."

I'm still upset that I wasn't at his side to help him. But eventually I realize that Dad's spirit wasn't caught up in the crazy chaos going on in the hospital room. He was with me, and he was clearly happy and free! I'm grateful that I was sitting in meditation and able to see him so clearly.

Days later, as family gathers in the living room to discuss funeral arrangements, my three-year-old daughter runs into the room and stops suddenly. "Why is everyone crying?" she asks, looking around at our sad faces.

"Because Grandpa died and we miss him," says my brother Tom.

"I just saw him fly past the window and he looked happy," she says with absolute innocence—looking at us, confused, as if we've got it wrong.

My brother kneels in front of her and says gently, "Tell me what you saw, Sarah."

She describes my father looking young and happy—flying past the window and waving to her. It makes us all smile to imagine it. We believe her. It helps us.

Another Story . . .

It's been a day that I'll have forever etched into my soul—July 13, 1980—the day my husband died. After our year long battle with colon cancer, Paul has slipped gracefully from his body, through my arms, and out to soar in the summer rain of a Colorado afternoon.

After weeks of exhausting medical traumas, I've come home from the hospital to sleep in our bed that now lives in the center of the living room. This bed is where we first shared love and dreams of the future—and finally morphine drips and nasogastric canisters that marked the end of Paul's life. At age thirty-five, he's gone.

His death has given me a gift of unquestionable awareness that we're souls on a journey and that life continues beyond the physical realms. But still he's gone. I'm widowed and alone at age twenty-nine. I already miss him.

Exhausted, I fall asleep in our bed and soon become aware that Paul is sleeping beside me. Of course he's here. He's my husband and I can feel his warm fuzzy legs wrapped around mine. I feel him embracing me tightly and feel his breath on my hair. I can't remember where he's been—but he's home now.

After a while, a man dressed in white stands beside the bed. I think he must be a nurse. His long arm stretches over me to tap Paul. Slowly

I realize he isn't wearing white and he isn't a nurse. He's emanating light. And he isn't human—but something else. I'm not sure what. As he reaches over me, Paul suddenly vanishes from beside me.

I open my eyes to see that it's 2 a.m., no one sleeps beside me, and no one stands beside the bed, dressed in white. I feel the unmistakable presence of a divine being. I realize Paul was here and a higher being came to move him on. His brief visit is over and his spirit guide is helping him move to the higher realms.

For several more nights, I'm awakened suddenly out of deep sleep—sensing a presence in the room. When I open my eyes, the clock reads the same time: 2 a.m. His visit is over.

A Client's Departed Mother Sends a Message

It's 2011 and my eyes are closed in meditation as I prepare to work with a client by phone. I can hear a persistent female voice in my ear saying: "I'm watching over my girls, having tea with them. Having tea with my girls . . ."

My client's name is Marya and she's thirty-four years old. During the phone session, I learn she's struggling with depression and can't get her career headed in the right direction. She hates her job.

The other woman's voice is still persistent in my ear. I describe the voice and the message to my client. "It's my mother!" says Marya. "She died suddenly ten years ago in a car accident. I have one sister. We were 'Mom's girls.' We had tea with her every day when we were little. When we were older, she'd invite us over for tea and conversation."

I describe the persistent, almost obnoxious energy of this woman I heard speaking into my ear. "Yes, that's my mom," she says.

Her mother's death marked a terrible turning point for Marya. She was twenty-four years old when it happened and never got over the sudden loss. It launched her into a major depression. "Why did my mom die so horribly? I needed her," cries Marya. "When it happened, I decided the world was a dark place and I didn't want to be here. Nothing made sense anymore."

As we talk, a ray of sunlight shines through my office window onto the wall across from me. The sunlight, dappled by the moving leaves outside my window, creates a distinct shadow on the wall. It's a perfect picture of a beautiful woman's face. I describe this face to Marya. It's her mom.

For the entire hour of our phone session, I stare at the perfect image of the woman's face on the wall. The face has never appeared before or since in my office. My client's mother was so determined that I give Marya a message that she manifested a distinct image of herself for me to see.

"Your mother is still with you, watching over you," I tell Marya. "You have to live like you know she's watching. Make her proud of you."

By the end of our session, Marya's voice is lighter. She agrees to take several baby steps toward doing her great work and fulfilling her soul's mission.

How Our Dreams Can Heal Us

Many times when I've been in pain, a departed loved one has come into my dreams to heal me. I first published this story about my friend Crissie in my book *I See Your Soul Mate,* and received so many e-mails from people telling me how the story helped them. I'm putting it into this book too, in hopes it inspires you to connect with someone you've lost.

I met my lifelong best girlfriend, Crissie, in second grade on the swing set of our Catholic elementary school playground. Her crazy brilliance and insane wit bonded us immediately. Our first conversation went something like this (although she was doing all the talking): "Don't you think the word 'nunnery' is weird, like a cannery? Why would a girl choose to be canned . . . er . . . nunned? Do you think nuns all come out the same from a nunnery like peas from a cannery? What if Shakespeare said, 'Get thee to a cannery!'" As she talked, she cracked herself up, bending over in peals of giggles that had me laughing uncontrollably along with her. I realized I had found a true friend—someone who thought outside the box. I didn't always understand her, but I loved her instantly.

Years later, in seventh grade, the Beatles appeared on *Ed Sullivan*. Crissie and I were the only ones in our Catholic elementary school to have our lives changed at that moment. We knew the Beatles meant more than wonderful music and that they were showing us a bigger, more exciting life that we both wanted. We promised each other that we'd get out of the South as soon as we graduated high school and fulfill our huge dreams. She never let me forget that promise.

Her brilliance put her at the top of every class and got her accepted into Georgetown University in 1969 as one of a small group of the first women ever accepted to that prestigious college in Washington, D.C.

When I told her I had been accepted into University of Missouri to study journalism, she forever called it "University of Misery" and told me I should have "aimed for a coast." (She was right! But I wasn't as smart as she was, so I was grateful for the chance to attend University of Misery.)

Our friendship lasted long beyond my stint at Misery and hers at Georgetown. Her first true love had been a fellow student at Georgetown University named Paul Frederick, to whom she became engaged. Two months before the big Southern wedding her parents had happily planned, Paul Frederick dumped her. Crissie never truly got over it.

Later when I moved to Colorado and met a handsome mountaineer named Paul Frederick (not the same guy), I was immediately leery of him. Would he break my heart too? (Turns out he did.) Crissie was the first friend to come visit us and meet my new love, whose name was the same as that of the man who broke her heart. She liked him right away.

When my Paul Frederick was diagnosed with cancer, Crissie's frequent phone calls helped me cope. With Crissie, every conversation was about exploring new ideas, asking tough questions, and searching for the truth—all done in a gleefully witty way. I adored her. She asked me the toughest questions anyone ever did. And she made me laugh harder than anyone I knew. She always told me I was a gifted writer and should "just write, dammit!"

Six months after Paul died, Crissie came to visit. She cheered me up and challenged me simultaneously. What was I doing with my life now? Was I moving forward? Was I writing? She prodded and poked as we drove to the mountains to ski. She seemed healthy, energetic, lonely as usual, but generally happy with her California graduate student lifestyle. (She was getting a PhD in botany.)

On her flight back home to California, she noticed bruises appearing on her body. By the time she landed in San Francisco, she was covered in bruises and rushed by ambulance to the hospital. Her stunning leukemia diagnosis so soon after Paul's death was overwhelming. After this devastating news, I suffered several anxiety attacks where my throat would tighten up and I couldn't swallow or eat. I felt nauseated most of the time.

Crissie's mother moved to California to take care of her, and her father got her into the most advanced treatment of the time—a bone marrow transplant at Fred Hutchinson Hospital in Seattle. Surrounded by friends and family, she went through chemo and radiation treatments and nearly died during the torturous bone marrow transplant. I couldn't understand why someone as bright, loving, and good as Crissie would have to go through such suffering—as horrible as Paul's experience. In deep despair and grief, I sold my belongings and moved to Mexico to teach fitness at a resort. I needed healing and was dropping out of a world that made no sense anymore.

When Crissie was finally in remission, she moved back to California and resumed graduate school studies. But she was only thirty-one years old and had been through hell. She was in a deep spiritual crisis, wondering what the purpose of life was. I understood her pain.

We stayed in touch with letters and phone calls. She began getting her life going again and started to feel better. She yelled at me when I told her I was in love with a married (but separated) Mexican man named Emilio who ran the local dive shop. "Sue Ellen, you'll only get your heart broken! You're a writer, so you can use it in something I guess . . . but really. Come back home and write, dammit!" I couldn't go home yet. My peaceful life of snorkeling and diving every day with Emilio was a form of healing for me—even if I knew Emilio would never be my lifelong partner. I loved him anyway.

Crissie and I made a plan to see each other back on our childhood turf. Crissie flew to the Gulf Coast to visit her family at the same time I flew home to visit mine. Our dads both owned fishing boats and had beach houses. Crissie's dad brought her over to the harbor near our beach house to spend time with us. My dad (who loved Crissie) took us fishing and boating. When we got bored with fishing, he dropped us off at a remote island to talk while he fished around the island.

Crissie and I walked and talked for hours along the sandy shore and crystal-clear water of our tiny remote island. We talked about her ongoing struggle with leukemia, her bone marrow transplant, her feelings about death, my grief over Paul, my attempts to end my ill-fated relationship with Emilio, and her heartbreaking belief that she would never find a soul mate or have children. She felt alone and unlovable. "What's the hardest part?" I asked her. "Disappointing my dad," she said as tears flowed. "He wants me to live so badly. . . ." I knew then that she was dying, no matter what the doctors said. I recognized the process of letting go that she was experiencing. It was the same conversation I'd had with Paul.

When my dad picked us up on the island, he took us back to the marina, where Crissie's dad waited on his fishing boat. As our dads laughed and joked with each other, Crissie and I hugged one last time. She couldn't look me in the eye as she turned away and stepped onto her dad's boat. As their boat moved out of the harbor, Crissie and I waved. When she was out of view, I broke down in uncontrollable sobs. My dad gently asked, "Why are you so sad? She looks great. She's going to make it." I turned to him crying and said, "Dad, this is the last time I'll ever see her. I know it." Crissie returned to her home in California. I returned to Mexico. Three months later she was dead.

The night of her death, before I knew she had died, Crissie came to me in my dreams. We spent the entire night laughing and giggling together (the way she and I always did). When I woke up, my stomach muscles were actually sore from laughing so hard. I've never before or since experienced such physical sensations after a dream as I did from that night with Crissie.

That morning as I was making coffee and about to call the States and check in with Crissie, I got the phone call telling me she had died during the night. I realized she had visited me in my dreams to let me know she was fine and to tell me that death wasn't the end of anything.

But Crissie wasn't done teaching me yet. A year later, I was finally back living in the States, heartbroken over Emilio, and trying to get my life and career on track. My grief over the loss of Crissie, Paul, and Emilio was weighing me down with sadness and depression.

One night, Crissie came to me in a dream and healed my heartbreak. In the dream, Crissie and I are standing on a white stone balcony overlooking an emerald green sea. It's peaceful and extraordinarily beautiful, and I feel so content standing beside her. We're talking as we always did but not using words. She's standing a bit behind me and to my left as we look out over the water. I notice that her physical body is shimmering and seems to be more like dappled light than a fully formed physical presence. The form that I know as Crissie is changing. Her hand is on my back, rubbing it in circles while she talks to me. We're discussing my heartbreak over Emilio.

She pulls out several handwritten letters on many different pieces of stationery that Emilio had written to his estranged wife (who lived in another city during our relationship). In the letters, Emilio is professing his undying love for his wife. Page after page contains stories of how well his diving business is going and how wonderful their life will be when he returns home to her. Crissie makes it clear to me that Emilio never really loved me, and I have to let him go and move on. As she shows me these letters, my pain and grief from all my losses well up in my chest. While she rubs my back, a loud wailing cry escapes me; the sound soars across the emerald sea in front of us. It's powerful, ancient, and deep—louder than any sound I've ever made. As this pain pours out of me and flows across the water, Crissie lovingly rubs my back and encourages me to let it all go.

When I've finished crying, Crissie slowly disappears beside me. I wake up still hearing the sound of my painful wailing and feeling Crissie's hand on my back. I cry most of the morning. But as the days go by, I realize that my grief has subsided. Finally I'm able to begin a journey of reinvention and spiritual exploration that pushes me toward the work I do today.

Chapter Two

HOW SPIRITS TRY TO CONNECT WITH YOU

Found Objects

In my daily work with clients, I've heard hundreds of stories about grieving people finding an object that they believe is a sign from their departed loved one. These experiences are always very healing for the grieving person—a moment that helps them understand that their loved one lives on and watches over them.

On Valentine's Day, seven months after Paul died, I was going through a filing cabinet, looking for financial information to prepare my taxes, when I discovered a chocolate Valentine heart with a ribbon wrapped around it and a note from Paul wishing me, *Happy Valentine's Day.* It stunned me to find it.

As I sat on the floor, crying and amazed to be holding a Valentine's gift from my dead husband on Valentine's Day, I remembered that one year ago, Paul had said he couldn't find a little Valentine's gift he'd bought me. He was frustrated that he couldn't remember where he'd put it. One year later, seven months after his death, he nudged me to find it where he'd left it. He helped me find it exactly on Valentine's Day.

These impossible events are not coincidences. They're our loved ones reaching out to help us heal and to show us that we're not alone. Take a moment to reflect on when this may have happened in your life. Do you remember finding something that you knew in your heart was a gift from your departed? Honor them by acknowledging you received it and knew it was from them. Say, "Thank you, I recognize your divine presence in my life."

Pam Porter's Story
I grew up just outside Santa Fe, New Mexico, and used to take daily walks behind our house with my mom. My mom had a strong affinity for Native Americans and the Old West and frequently found arrowheads hidden on the trails behind our house. She kept the arrowheads in a small box on her dresser and we loved looking at them together. I was quite envious of her beautiful collection and wished that I could find an arrowhead too. I never found one—until the first anniversary of her death.

My wonderful mother passed away from cancer in August of 2004. The first year after her death was especially difficult for me, and even though I felt like she was still around, I really missed her and was incredibly sad much of the time. For me the world had turned upside down and life would never be the same.

On the anniversary of her death, I was walking along a popular trail outside Boulder, Colorado, where I now live. Halfway through the walk, I happened to look down at just the right moment and I saw a large, perfect arrowhead sitting on top of the path. It looked like someone had just placed it there.

I instantly knew that it was a gift from my mother and that she was letting me know that she was close by and that she was okay. The heavy grief that I had experienced that year finally shifted.

I still have the arrowhead, and it is a constant reminder to me that death is an illusion, and that loved ones who have passed on are still with us.

Signs in Nature
When your loved one crosses over, they'll often manifest signs in nature to let you know that they're still watching over you. Yet we frequently dismiss these signs as meaningless. How frustrating this must be to

our loved ones on the other side! They reach out to comfort us and we dismiss it as coincidence.

When Paul and I were falling in love, he gave me a beautiful silver necklace and matching earrings with a jade moon and star pendant. The necklace pendant and each earring featured a crescent moon with a star in the middle of the crescent. He told me that he was the moon and I was his shining star. This became the symbol of our love, and I wore the necklace every day. Many times during our relationship he whispered to me, "You're my shining star."

Three days after his death on July 13, we held an outdoor memorial service in our backyard. It was a clear beautiful summer evening in the mountains. A group of about thirty friends sat in a large circle, sharing Paul stories.

In the middle of this heartfelt evening, a friend nudged me to look up at the sky. Directly above us was the crescent moon with a bright star (Jupiter) in the middle of the crescent—exactly reflecting the image in the pendant Paul had given me, which I was wearing that evening. I shared this uncanny sign with our friends and passed around my necklace for everyone to see. The pendant was duplicated in the sky above our heads.

We all felt a rush of energy and knew that Paul was with us. It was a healing moment for everyone in the group—a sense of his presence and a sign of divine order in action.

Later I learned that the sky configuration with Jupiter nestled inside the crescent moon rarely occurs. I don't believe in coincidences. Imagine how many factors were in motion to line up that exact astronomical configuration (which had always symbolized our relationship) on the night I would be sitting outside, mourning his loss with my friends at his memorial service. Divine order is so much greater than we can imagine.

Here's a story from my cousin Linda about getting a sign in nature from her departed parents.

A Letter from My Cousin: Linda Long's Story

Hello, Cousin Sue! As you know, I've grieved the loss of my wonderful parents and had great difficulty believing that life carried on beyond this world. But recently, my husband, Rob; my brother Peter; his wife, Kim; and I took a trip of lifetime to the ancient cities, beginning in Rome, going to Turkey, Israel, and Egypt.

On the evening of September 4, we went to see the pyramids with our tour group of about one hundred people. We were all sitting in the desert, facing the great pyramids with the Sphinx directly in front of us. It was quite dark out and the stars were beautiful. A new moon was setting behind the largest pyramid, and the outlines of the other pyramids were vivid against the night sky.

Suddenly I saw the largest meteorite I have ever seen in my life; it streaked across the sky above the pyramids, vividly lighting up the dark night. It was breathtaking.

My brother Peter turned to me and said, "Did you see that?" I said, "Yes!" But we asked around us and no one else had seen this extraordinary display of light across the night sky. Neither my husband sitting beside me, nor Peter's wife sitting beside him, nor any of the people sitting near us had seen anything. I asked all around when we were leaving, and also asked the people on our tour bus, if any of them had seen the enormous meteorite streak across the sky. But not one of them had seen it, Sue! Out of more than a hundred people, only my brother Peter and I saw the brilliant meteorite streak across the night sky.

And as I was getting on the tour bus the following day, someone pointed out that I had a ladybug on my blouse. Apparently, in the Middle East that means someone from "the other side" is sending you a message.

I am now a believer, Sue. Mom and Dad said hello to my brother Peter and me that night, and they let us know that all was well. And they did it in a way that we couldn't ignore. I think you've finally convinced your very skeptical cousin, a retired federal agent, that we can have communications from those who have passed. And I'm finally paying attention to the other side of my brain!

And now I'm having better dreams about my parents. I'm waking up at peace instead of anxious whenever I dream about them.

The Whisper You Most Often Ignore: Your Own Intuition

Because our culture highly values our left brain and its linear logical thought processes, we learn early in childhood that this is the important piece of the brain to develop—starting with words and language. We slowly learn to dismiss the right-brain impressions, visions, intuitions, and dreams that come to us so naturally in our early years.

As a result, by the time we've reached adulthood, many of us are no longer even aware that we're receiving information from the right brain. We've developed such a habit of giving priority to our left-brain linear thinking that we've silenced our intuition.

Yet our departed loved ones speak to us through these right-brain impressions, gut feelings, dreams, and images that we so easily dismiss.

There's a large body of scientific research validating intuition. My previous book *I See Your Soul Mate* cites much of it. You can learn more about the science behind intuition in books such as *The Conscious Universe* and *Entangled Minds* by Dean Radin, PhD. As director at the Institute of Noetic Sciences for more than two decades, Radin has conducted psychic research in academia at Princeton University, University of Edinburgh, University of Nevada, and in three Silicon Valley think tanks, including SRI International.

It helps you heal to listen to the whispers of your departed loved ones—and embrace what your higher self knows to be true. The benefits of shifting into this right brain consciousness are enormous—especially when you're lost in the pain of grief.

Whenever we tap into our right-brain consciousness through meditation, getting quiet and shutting down the mental chatter, we feel our connection to the divine. This process opens the door for our departed to comfort and guide us.

Here is a story that illustrates how we can learn to listen, and how listening can heal us.

On the Beach . . .

Sitting at the water's edge, digging my hands into the warm sand, I'm grateful for the family reunion that offered me a respite from my grief-filled Colorado life. At the age of thirty, I've found myself widowed, alone, and still traumatized from a year spent caring for a dying husband. My writing career has not been successful in the year since Paul died. And I need to find a job.

The sound of the waves is relentless and a welcome relief from my worry-filled thoughts. It feels good to cry and I let it happen—lying back against the sand. "I need to know why this happened and what I'm supposed to do now," I say out loud.

After exhausting myself from crying, I slip in and out of sleep to the rhythm of the crashing waves.

After a while I hear a familiar voice say, "Hey, I'm with you."

"Uh . . . What?" I say, sitting up and looking around startled— trying to determine if the voice is in my head or if someone is standing beside me on the beach.

The voice continues from deep inside, "Don't you feel my presence in your life?"

The energy of Paul, my departed husband, is all around me now, and the voice is clearly his. "I need you, Paul," I whisper. "I don't know how to survive here. I'm barely paying the rent. Why didn't you stay? You promised—"

"You needed that promise to keep you going. It was my job to support you through your greatest challenge. I held up my end. Don't you remember our agreement?" he asks gently.

"That was *my* greatest challenge? I thought it was yours," I say, remembering the exhausting year of medical emergencies, endless doctors, healers, and horrifying medical procedures.

"Yeah . . . something like that."

"You told me a million times that you would beat it and we'd have our future."

"I haven't broken my promise," he says. "Listen to what I'm saying. Our agreement is so much older than that. Can you remember another time? Can you remember being with me in a different world, making an agreement?"

"It hurts too much . . . ," I say, looking down at the sand.

"Don't disappoint me. You looked into my eyes long ago and said, 'I agree to love and release you—so that we can evolve and accomplish our missions.' We made this agreement in joy. Feel it. Remember it. It doesn't live in your logical mind. It lives in your higher self."

"I've lost my higher self," I mumble. But I'm trying hard to understand the things he's saying. For a while, all I can hear is the pounding of the waves.

"Sue, I'm counting on you to remember this agreement, or everything we went through is in vain. It was all to help us burn up our old patterns that we couldn't break any other way. Where's your highest self now? Where's my shining star?"

I'm quiet now. My tears have stopped. I'm getting a memory—a dreamlike vision. It's just as he described. We're making an agreement while looking into each other's eyes. But we're in a different world—far different from this one.

"Okay, maybe I can remember. But what do I do now? I need to make a living, and my writing isn't making money," I say, gazing out across the waves.

"You're the strong one who said you would stay and do the hard work after I left. You agreed to that. On our last day, I told you that you were gifted. Remember? But this person I see wrapped in sorrow and sitting on the sand feeling pitiful is not who I made that agreement with."

"I'm sorry," I whisper. "I've let us both down."

"Sue, you can feel the truth. Trust yourself. Do the work you came to do. I can't do it for you. You came to help raise consciousness. You're a brave, wise soul and this is what you agreed to."

I can feel his energy beginning to pull away.

"How do I help raise consciousness when I can hardly pay the rent?"

He says quietly, "You won't let me down. I know this about you. You'll remember."

"I feel so disconnected from this world . . . so empty."

"I'm with you. But you drown me out with your pain. Promise me you'll do better. Tell me you'll trust your inner voice."

"I'll try. I promise." I feel Paul slip away. After a while I lie back on the sand and stare into the enormous ocean sky, remembering.

I've always been strong. I know that. But I haven't lived that way lately. If my strength is on purpose and Paul's message is real— and not something I imagined—what do I do now? What do I do next?

I hear an inner whisper saying, "Get up. Embrace your gift. Use it to help others. Keep writing—but tell a different story."

I sit for a little longer on the beach as the tide comes in and the sun lowers against the horizon. There's an early moon rising to the east. The crashing waves are comforting.

I've always known I was here to write something—but I haven't been good enough at it. Or maybe I'm writing the wrong stories. I've always been intuitive and seen things that others don't. How do I make my living from that?

I know I need to exercise my body—that always makes me feel better. "Okay," I say, standing up and brushing the sand from my clothes. "Just one step. Today I'll go for a little run."

As I begin to run on the beach after months of barely moving, I feel an old forgotten power opening up inside. My thoughts shift from endless worry to a new plan of action. "When I get home," I tell myself, "I'll take that writing course I've wanted to take. I'll become better at meditation, maybe find a teacher. "

After a few days of running, I can feel a shift in my heart. I'm not so angry anymore. Layers of depression are lifting. I can feel it in my body. I feel lighter and can hear the guidance of something bigger when I'm quiet. In my daily meditations, I can sometimes hear Paul's voice.

It's just a beginning. But soon, I'm enrolled in journalism school and learning to make my living as a writer. Daily meditation eases my pain and helps me own my intuition. Those small steps eventually get me where I am today.

Chapter Three

CLIENT STORIES OF THEIR DEPARTED

When I began writing this book, I asked my clients if they had any stories to share about communicating with their departed loved ones. I was overwhelmed by the amazing stories they sent and wanted to share them with you.

Berry Fowler's Story

My brother, Brian Prescott Fowler, was born on the evening of my fifth birthday. He was from then on referred to as my greatest birthday present. Over the next twenty-five years, my baby brother often endured the tortures and sometimes the benefits of having a brother five years his senior. And, although I loved him dearly, it really wasn't until about the time I turned thirty that we became best friends.

Brian was a huge man with an even bigger heart. If you're old enough to remember the character Hoss Cartwright, played by Dan Blocker on the long-running hit television series Bonanza, *you'll have almost known my brother Brian. Hoss and Brian were cut from the same cloth, wearing their hearts on their sleeves, standing up for others, and giving much more than they took.*

Brian and I did everything together. From meeting Friday afternoons for happy hour, to our monthly Costco runs, to the occasional late-night call when one of our cars wouldn't start, we counted on each other.

On July 16, 2010, Brian died suddenly because of complications from a combination of diabetes and recently diagnosed leukemia. He was fifty-eight. He had called me that morning at 11:20, asking if I would take him to the hospital because he was having trouble breathing. By six that evening, Brian had passed away. I was devastated. My wife and children were devastated. Brian's friends were devastated. One of the brightest lights in all our lives would no longer shine.

Over the next year, there was not a day, perhaps not even an hour, when I didn't think of Brian. On the morning of July 16, 2011, the first anniversary of my brother's death, I woke with a jolt. I'd seen Brian vividly in my dreams. I was standing in a room with two open doors—one straight in front of me and one on the right. Suddenly, Brian walked past me on the left and straight through the door in front of me. He had a look of determination on his face as he passed by. Although he said nothing and we didn't meet eye to eye, I felt he knew I was there. The other thing I noticed was how good he looked. He was thinner and younger, and there was a definite spring in his step. As I was turning to call out to him, I caught another peek of him as he passed by the open door to my right —heading back in the direction he had come from.

It was an amazing dream and I felt happy and blessed for having it.

But what followed later that day surprised me even more.

Later that morning, I was on the telephone, sitting at my desk and sharing my dream with my business partner, Barbara Wainwright. Barbara and I own a company that trains and certifies life and business coaches, and besides being business partners, we are good friends. Barbara's specialty is spiritual coaching, so she was quite excited to hear about my dream. And although my specialty had always been business coaching, after working with Barbara for the past four years, I had become much more open to the possibility that my dream may have truly been a visit from my brother.

As Barbara and I were talking, I kept looking at a framed piece of art by Western artist Bob Moline that hangs directly across from my desk.

The picture is titled Medicine Feather, *and it depicts a Native American holding a white feather as he kneels in prayer. I had inherited this picture from my brother, Brian. One of the things that made it very special was that our father, Walt Fowler, had been the model for the man in the picture. Our father had been a practicing medicine man and was well known for his sweat ceremonies.*

After I finished my call with Barbara, I was walking downstairs to make lunch when I heard a loud clap of thunder. I love thunderstorms. When I was a child growing up in Texas and Oklahoma, my whole family would gather on the back porch to watch the great storms that would roll through our area. It was always a memorable event and something that my brother and sister and I continued to enjoy throughout our lives.

Not wanting to miss this storm, I rushed outside to watch the show. To my surprise, the sky was only partly cloudy and the sun was shining brightly. And although it had sprinkled a bit earlier, there was no rain falling. As I turned to go back inside, I noticed a white feather stuck to the driver's side of my truck. The feather, very similar to the one in the painting that our father had modeled for, was perfectly shaped, delicate, and beautiful. It's a gift from my brother that I'll never forget.

Isabella Cappucci's Story

I grew up feeling loved and nurtured by my aunt Emma (Tía Emma) in a way that I never experienced with my own mother. My mother and I always had a very troubled and hurtful relationship. Last year, these two sisters, my mother and my aunt, both passed away within months of each other. I grieved terribly for Tía Emma. A few months ago, I had a dream that was significant.

In my dream, I was sitting at our kitchen table with my sister and cousin, and we were looking out my mother's window. All of a sudden, my mother and Tía Emma appeared. They were both wearing traditional long Mexican dresses with embroidered flowers on the front and on the cap sleeves. My aunt's dress was colorful—bright yellow and orange. My mother's dress was black.

My aunt appeared to be much younger than when she died. But my mother still looked old and tired, as she did about five years ago—with her platinum-dyed hair brushed back. My aunt's left hand was holding my mother's right elbow—as though my tía were actually bringing my mother to see me. My mother looked uncertain and afraid, as though she didn't want to come any closer.

I gasped and jumped up from my seat to greet them with open arms. My mother saw this, took a huge sigh of relief, and gave me an enormous smile. When we hugged, I said, "Oh, Mom!" We both broke down and cried. I felt forgiveness pass between us. The most fascinating part of this dream was that I actually physically felt *the hug in my dream as though it were really happening!*

In the moment that we hugged, my mother suddenly appeared petite and cute, as she did when she was in her twenties and thirties. And her black Mexican smock transformed into a beautiful shimmery silver lamé gown. A golden hat appeared on her head—square at the top with flowing netting that fell to her shoulders.

This dream was very significant to me and marked a major turning point in my recovery. I feel my tía *brought my mother to me for forgiveness. My* tía *always knew the pain I carried from feeling abandoned and rejected by my mother. My* tía *and I had talked about it numerous times. When I woke up after our embrace, I felt immediately happy and at peace. And I felt* loved *by my mother.*

I believe this is truly the beginning of my healing journey between my mother and me. I now look at my mother with more compassion. Although she may not have possessed the soul capacity to love her children while she was alive, I do believe she loves and wants the best for us now. I don't know what troubled her in her own life here. But she must have been in a lot of pain and must have felt unloved and invalidated herself. I can see all that now and I feel only forgiveness and love toward her.

Kat Garrard's Story

My mom died of cancer when I was sixteen years old. The eighteen months prior to her death were a confused mess of my parents divorcing, moving away from our hometown with my dad, leaving our church, and watching my mom's decline because of cancer. I was caught in the middle of a devastating custody battle between my parents.

For a developing teenage girl, it was a disorienting and horrendous time. The loss of my beautiful mom was like having the stars and moon disappear from an already dark night. She was a devoted mom. She was witty, contemplative, creative, spiritual, and bold. She loved her children fully and fiercely.

A few weeks after losing custody of us, my mom died in her parents' home—hours away from her children. At her funeral, in shock at seeing her body, I reached out and touched her hand. Every cell in my body expected her to wake up. When she did not, my life stopped making sense.

A few years later, I returned to her gravesite. It was my first visit there without my dad and siblings. To the outside world, I had handled my mom's death well. In my heart, I had grieved alone and ashamed. I was full of anxiety about where my mom's spirit was and racked with secret guilt that I hadn't defied the custody order and run away to be with her at the end of her life. I knelt down in front of her gravestone and poured out my terrible feelings that I had choked down for so long. I sobbed so hard that I wondered if my broken heart would leave me dead beside her grave.

When the deepest wave of grief had passed and I was weak and open in a way I didn't know I was capable of being, I suddenly knew my mom was with me. It was the way the sun feels when it reaches down through a break in the clouds. I felt the warmth of her spirit and her love across my back. She was all around me, comforting and mothering me. I knew she was aware of every moment I'd had since her death. She assured me of the universal order of life and that she had departed her life as part of this divine order. Her message was that all was okay.

I was so young, I could not fully understand everything she was sharing with me and I wanted only to know what this meant for her. Was she at peace? Sensing this, she comforted me. She assured me she was happy and safe and not angry with me at all. She spent time cheering me up, nurturing me, and filling me with joy. I was able to be a child again for a short time there at her gravesite. She fortified my heart with strength and I eventually knew when it was time for her to go. When her presence left, I felt loved and at peace.

I had not physically seen her with me. I did not hear her in the usual way. Yet I have no doubt that I felt her and felt her words in the language of spirit. The greater concept of divine order was a gift from my mother that I would keep to open later in life. Since that day, I've had other moments of communication with departed loved ones and have developed a deepening spiritual path. On that profoundly healing day, though, I was able to stand up from my mother's grave and walk back into life, knowing that my beautiful mom was joyful and at peace and loved me as fully as I will always love her.

Joan Frederick's Story

Joan is the sister of my departed husband, Paul. This is one of her powerful stories.

For almost twenty years, I taught high school art classes ten to twelve hours per day, plus grading at home and fulfilling other teaching responsibilities. I became exhausted from the negative attitudes, especially in the administration. Eventually I was miserable at my job. But I had to endure to hit the magic number of years required so I could retire with benefits and a half salary guaranteed for life. I was in daily survival mode.

During the last three years of this ordeal, my beautiful mother passed away and I was left the lone survivor of my loving family of four. I missed them all terribly.

One night while still trying to survive my life as a public educator, I dreamed that I was in a room with friends and we were chatting and having fun. I looked across the hall and in another room my mother was sitting at a table, speaking to a man I didn't know. She had been dead about three years by then. In the dream, I asked my friends, "What's my mom doing in that room?" They said to me, "She's planning her daughter's funeral."

I thought to myself, "Oh, I should go over and help her." When she passed away, I was completely by myself, planning everything and taking care of her estate, and it was brutal. So I wanted to help her. But then I realized, "Hey, I'm her daughter!"

It upset me so much, I woke up from my dream and thought, "Oh no, I'm going to die!"

I drove to work that day, terrified of being killed in a car accident. But weeks turned into months and I began to wonder why I had dreamed that dream, since I was still alive and healthy.

As I thought about it, I began to realize that my job was killing me. And if I didn't get away from that negative environment, I would indeed die. So I began to make plans to quit my job, even though it meant my future would be uncertain and I wouldn't have the stable pension I had planned for all the years of my teaching career. I began to see that if I used the money I had inherited from the sale of my mother's house, I could reinvent myself into a portrait and art photographer and make money doing what I loved instead of working at a job that I hated and that was physically and emotionally draining me. It was scary, but I quit my job.

Now I'm doing what I envisioned doing when I left high school, happy to make my living as an artist. I knew then what I wanted to do, but so many obstacles and duties got in the way, including motherhood, survival mode thinking, and fear of not being good enough.

Thanks to my mom nudging me in a dream (she's still looking out for me), I'm now making my dreams come true and couldn't be happier. I'm a very lucky girl! And I'm not dead yet.

Judy Colburn's Story

My brother Mark committed suicide in 1999. We were very close. He was sixteen months older than me and from the moment I was born, he was my protector, the one who always looked out for me. There was nothing we would not do for one another and we were always there for each other.

I was absolutely devastated by his death. And I was very concerned about his soul being at peace. We were raised Catholic, so I worried that he might have gone to hell. I was taught that suicide was a mortal sin—a sin that God did not forgive.

At the time of his death, he was recently divorced and his two young daughters were living with him. I was the administrator of his estate. He had told me many times what he wanted to happen in the event of his death, and I was determined to carry out every single one of his wishes, at whatever cost.

My fears about him spending eternity in hell were calmed after meeting with the priest to make funeral arrangements. The priest explained that the Church had changed its thinking on suicide. I took great comfort in that.

During the days following Mark's death, I understood why Mark had taken his own life and I forgave him. But still, my grief was centered upon his emotional state in the afterlife. I desperately needed to know if he was at peace.

Several days after he died, my best friend Linda called me. She said she had had a dream about Mark. She was back East and I was in Arizona and I hadn't had any time to talk to her about my feelings. So what she told me amazed me. This is what she described:

Linda, Mark, and I were sitting on the floor in a circle. She said that Mark was dressed in dark slacks, a white shirt that was open at the collar, and he did not have any shoes on. She said no words were spoken but Mark was very relaxed, and after a while, he held up his hand and made a peace sign.

What was so amazing is that Linda described the exact clothing we had buried Mark in. And he hated wearing shoes, so we buried him with just socks on. I started crying because Linda did not know what clothes Mark was wearing when we buried him so I knew that through Linda, my brother was letting me know that he was indeed at peace. I can't begin to describe the relief that flooded through me, knowing that he was really okay.

A few months after he died, Mark visited me in a dream. I had so many questions for him. I remember this like it happened just now. We had a long conversation and he answered all my questions—even the ones about my future. And even though he was still angry at his ex-wife, he was mostly at peace. When I woke up after the dream, I could still feel his presence in the room.

Mark came to visit me again some time later. This time he was playful. In the dream, I was sitting on a couch in a room that had doorways at both ends. I was aware of someone running in and out of the doors—in a circle over and over again—trying to get my attention. I knew it was Mark and I started laughing. I said, "Mark, I know it's you. Come and talk to me."

He sat down and I began asking questions. I asked him if he'd seen God and he said yes. I asked him questions about the future again and he said, "I can't tell you anything." His tone suggested that he may have been "spoken to" about revealing the future last time. I asked him if he regretted taking his life. He said yes and that if he could go back, he would not have done it that way.

When I woke up, I could still feel Mark's presence with me. That's how I can tell the difference between a dream and a visit.

I had another dream visit not long after both my mom and grandmother passed away. I was sitting at a long table and my grandmother appeared. She was just sitting at the table. I was asking people if they could see her and they said they could. I was amazed because I wasn't the only one who could see her. Then my aunt appeared, then Mark. Several family members who had passed over were there. I didn't speak to any of them. I just saw them. I thought to myself, "Now all I need is Mom to be here." And I turned around and she was standing there, asking to have lunch with me.

I knew that the whole purpose of that dream was their way of telling me that they loved me and were watching over me.

Recently, because of an unsettling feeling I had about Mark, I needed to contact him. I needed to know if he was okay. I contacted a medium and she said that Mark needed someone in the family to forgive him. She said he could still feel their anger and that he felt really bad because he had no idea that his death would tear our family apart so badly. He said that certain family members were talking about him again, and he knew that someone had not forgiven him.

It was National Suicide Prevention Week and that had brought the conversation up again within our family. Mark had heard what people said and knew he had still not been forgiven by everyone. I hope they will forgive him so he can be at peace.

Wanda Morrison's Story

I was working at a supermarket as a cake decorator and met a very nice baker named Dave. One afternoon, I had scheduled a meeting with a psychic and mentioned to Dave that I was going to get my tarot cards read after work. He seemed interested but didn't say much. While I was having my cards read, the woman asked me if I knew a man who had lost a son—Michael? Dave? It was someone I worked with, she said.

I knew Dave had lost a son to cancer and his name was Michael. I said yes. She went on to tell me that I must get a message to Dave and let him know that his son does hear him and he is communicating with him and the conversations he has with him are real. She also told me that there was some sort of anniversary of his death coming up and that this information would help confirm this message.

The next day at work, I could hear my own guides clearly telling me I must give Dave the message. I didn't know Dave very well at the time, and I was hesitant to say anything to him. So I told my guides that I would give the message to Dave only if he asked me directly about the reading.

Right after I had that thought, Dave asked me, "So how was the reading?" I almost fell over. So I told him what the woman had told me. Dave stood still for a minute, listening. Then he turned red and broke down and cried. He hugged me and said that I had no idea how much this information meant to him. He had asked for a sign from his departed son, Mikey. And that afternoon he was going to an anniversary memorial event for his son at the school his son had attended.

Dave and I became very close friends after that. Dave is now a very powerful healer, and I will forever be humbled and touched by this story of love and connection. Each time I tell this story, I am again deeply moved by it.

Debi Brown's Story

This year, one of the most difficult things I'm facing is my mom's mental decline. She's about to turn eighty. I've been so very worried about her. She used to be strong and independent. On my last visit, she confided that she was frightened about her memory loss and her inability to do things she used to do easily. I reassured her as best I could, but I was weeping inside. What a horrible thing to face!

Not long after our visit, I had a Reiki energy session. During the session, I went into an altered state, where I was surrounded by lush green trees and grass. There was water nearby—a river, I think. It reminded me of what I imagine Ireland looks like. I kept hearing: "All is well. You are safe. You are loved."

A woman appeared who did not look familiar to me. But I knew it was my nana, my mom's mom! She passed away twenty years ago, at about the same age my mom is now. But in this vision she looked young—younger than I had ever known her to be— probably in her thirties or forties. She wore the glasses I recognized from her later years, and she had the same smile. She didn't actually speak. But she told me that I didn't need to worry so much about my mom, because she would always be with her.

At first I was very afraid, because I thought she was telling me my mom was going to die soon. But I kept hearing "All is well.

You are safe. You are loved." I knew with every fiber of my being that it was my nana (who was born in Ireland). And she was telling me to trust that my mom would be safe with her.

Since then, my mom has been diagnosed with dementia. I think Nana wanted to reassure me that my mom wouldn't ever be alone on her journey. The vision I received was an amazing and mind- blowing experience. And it was a tremendous gift. I've been able to make peace with my mom's condition and be comforted, knowing that Nana is always with her.

Another Story from Joan Frederick, My Departed Husband's Sister
I spent ten years working on a biography of a famous Native American artist, Kiowa painter T. C. Cannon. After ten years of dedicated research, interviewing, and several rewrites, all to honor the life and work of a man I'd never met, the book was finally published.

T.C. had died young at the age of thirty-one. His sister Joyce was managing his estate. After my book about T.C. came out, I helped Joyce navigate the business of marketing and selling T.C.'s paintings.

One hot summer day, after we'd spent eight hours sorting through the remains of his estate, it was obvious that Joyce was tired and wanted to leave. But I knew that T.C.'s extensive library of books by the artists, writers, and philosophers who shaped his work were stored in the small, broken-down shed out in the yard. I had spent time there years before, doing research for my book.

I asked her, "What about T.C.'s library? You could send those books that he loved to the students at the Institute of American Indian Arts." The IAIA is the school in Santa Fe where T.C. became famous and honed his craft. Joyce was tired and not feeling well. She told me that I could give the books to the kids, but she needed to go home.

I had about three hours of daylight left, so I walked out into the hot Oklahoma sun to survey the shed where I had once spent days researching.

I opened the door and peered inside. The dust and spiderwebs were everywhere, but nothing had been touched since I had left there years earlier. Even the saucer I left sitting on the cabinet was untouched. It was spooky.

I began to pile the books into my car, one by one. The dust was choking me. The outside temperature was reaching 102 degrees and I was scared of being bitten by the numerous spiders and scorpions.

Sweating and filthy from the dust and cobwebs, I piled every book for the students at the IAIA into my car. Exhausted, I drove two hours to get home, shower, and fall asleep.

That night I dreamed about T.C. all night. I was following him around a large city. I would walk down a street and ask a bystander, "Have you seen T.C.?" And they would point down the street and say, "Yes, he just passed by here and went that way."

I traveled different avenues, asking the same question and getting various answers, all telling me he was just over the horizon.

Then I turned into an alley and came to a dead end. I looked around, wondering where he could have gone, and saw a large staircase climbing up the side of a building to a small door many flights above me.

I slowly climbed up the rickety stairs. When I reached the top, it was so bright. It was like the sun was right behind my head. There was white, hot light pouring all around me. As I stood there in the light, I noticed a door.

I went inside. At first, I couldn't see anything as my eyes tried to adjust to the room after being outside in the white light. I closed the door slightly and tried to get my bearings. Behind the door was a fairly large pile of Indian dance regalia with bustles, leggings, beadwork, and rattles all wrapped up in plastic with a small paper sign taped to it that said: T.C.

I thought to myself, "Great! T.C. must be in here!" I looked around the room because my eyes were beginning to adjust to the dimmer light, and I saw T.C. lying on a couch over by the wall. He was lying on his side, propped up on one elbow.

He was wearing the outfit that he had painted onto the figure of his most famous painting: Man in a Wicker Chair. *The only difference was that he had on the dark plastic framed glasses that he had worn as a young student at the Institute of the American Indian Arts in the 1960s.*

He looked straight at me and said, "I'm glad those kids at IAIA are going to get those books." Then I woke up.

I sacrificed greatly to write T.C.'s biography because I respected him and his work. And it may not be true, but I believe he visited me that night to thank me for my efforts. I cannot tell you how happy I was when I woke up.

Joan Frederick's book, *T. C. Cannon: He Stood in the Sun,* was published by Northland Publishing in 1995.

Charlene Ellington's Story
I knew the Estings family my entire life, and when I was thirteen years old, my family moved just up the street from them. Of their three children, Ryan was my age. But it was his older sister Mary that I spent a lot of time with and was the closest to. I spent many afternoons and weekends at their home.

Five years ago, I unexpectedly ran into Mary after not seeing her for many years. I was surprised when she shared that her brother Ryan had committed suicide. She was so distraught; Ryan had overdosed on painkillers and left a suicide note.

Three years later, Ryan visited me in a dream and was adamant that I tell Mary that he did not kill himself on purpose and that he was sorry. He visited me several additional times, insisting that I tell her. But I didn't know where she was, so all I could do was promise him that I would tell her if I ever saw her.

Last summer on a Wednesday night, he appeared to me again in a dream. He looked like he was in his thirties, even though he was in his fifties at the time of his death. He seemed so real, vivid, and beautiful to me. In my dream, I was so happy to see him and hugged and hugged him. He felt so alive. It wasn't until I awoke that I realized that he had died five years ago. It felt more like an actual visit than a dream.

The following Monday, I was attending the graveside service of a relative when I turned around and there was Mary. It was the first time I'd seen her in years. I began hearing Ryan's voice incessantly in my ear, reminding me of what to tell her.

After the service, I took her aside and shared that Ryan had come to me several times since his death and he wanted her to know that he had not committed suicide intentionally—that he had been confused. She instantly began to weep. She asked why he had left a suicide note. I told her that his life was chaotic at the time and he was heavily drugged. He wanted her to know that he absolutely had not intended to die and hurt the family. He said that when it took place, he had been in great pain and was lost. He was very sorry and did not mean to hurt her or their family.

I told her that he especially wanted her to know that she was a good sister and he loved her very much. She wept the whole time I spoke with her, and she said through her tears that she loved him too. She said she'd been so angry with him since his suicide and that her life had been off track ever since. She had not been able to get over his death. I told her I hoped she would be able to find peace now, knowing that he was at peace and that he loved her. We sat talking long after everyone else had left the graveside services that day. Although Ryan had wanted her to know these things, I wasn't sure if it would cause her more grief when I brought it up. She assured me that she was grateful for the information and would try to forgive him and move on with her life. I haven't heard from Ryan since that day.

Lisa Livingstone's Story

When someone who has died comes to you in your dreams, it's an experience that's never forgotten. My experience was vivid and gave me a profound clarity that my mother was reaching out to me from the other side. The dream came one week after she died suddenly at age sixty-five from heart failure. It was only months after my brother Richard, her son, had died from AIDS.

I was very close to my mother. My siblings often remind me that I was the favorite child. Mom and I used to talk about how we felt like sisters or best friends. The dream that came the week after she died was intense. In the dream, my mom was speaking to me in great emotional pain: "I'm sorry. I didn't mean to leave you. I know you're so sad because of Richard. I didn't mean to leave you girls."

I awoke terrified and gasping for air. At the time, I was frightened by the dream and didn't fully recognize how her dream visit had helped me to heal my grief. Just the fact that Mom had reached out to me was a great comfort. The dream helped me realize that our love and relationship were always present and was eternal. I was deeply comforted by the fact that my mom was still with me. From then on, I felt her protecting me. She took on an angel's role in my life—especially when I went through hard times.

Since being invited to write this story, my father has been diagnosed with some serious health issues. This week while I was on the phone with my sisters, I saw my mom from the corner of my eye. It was a glimmer, but it was clearly her. She was letting me know that she's still here to care for her family and support Dad through his transition. It comforted me to see her.

Deb Davis's Story

Early December, three years ago, I was called home with news that doctors had discovered cancer in my father's stomach. When I arrived exhausted in his hospital room, I was stopped in my tracks at the door. Ringing the ceiling were about a dozen angels, hovering. Their energy was peaceful and loving. They had a calming effect on me.

I spent the last eighteen days of my dad's life with him in that hospital room, ceiling ringed with angels. I was the only one who saw them. I knew that the angels had arrived to help my dad overcome his fear of dying.

On the morning of my dad's death, my sister met me outside the hospital room, and her face was ashen. "Dad's dying," she said. When my dad took his last breath that day, family members burst into tears. But I watched in awe as a huge spirit poured out from the top of my dad's head and filled the space just below the ceiling. It was the spirit of my father; he was radiant and ecstatic! I felt a surge of love from him stronger than any love I had ever experienced from him before. I burst into tears of joy and gratitude.

My mother had died a couple years previously. Immediately after my father died, both my parents started showing up in my life and in my dreams—sending me bursts of unconditional love that would bring me to tears. I had never experienced that kind of love from them while they were alive. But I feel it now. I feel very blessed by this experience.

Dolores Rollins's Story

Two days before 9/11, I had a vivid dream of watching a huge fire, a catastrophe, and feeling powerless. In the dream, I walked through ankle-deep ash, picking up bones. Two days later, I saw that exact scene played out on the television news coverage of the attack on the World Trade Center.

The day after 9/11, I was driving my kids to school and looked in the rearview mirror and saw a man in his late twenties or early thirties stretched out comfortably in the back, smiling at the hubbub of my three young kids on their way to school. Then he disappeared.

Unbeknownst to me at this time, my brother had lost a close friend who worked for Cantor Fitzgerald in the Twin Towers. When my sister later showed me his picture, it was the exact man who had been in the backseat. Why he chose to visit me, I still don't know. But he was clearly happy and at peace.

Cindy Covington's Story

In the late '80s, my mother's brother John passed away from cancer. He was in his forties at the time of his passing. During his life, he was a master auto painter who liked beer, cigars, and fine steaks. He was renowned in the Southern California area for his craft and had many celebrity clients. He did not have such good luck with relationships and had just finalized his second divorce at the time of his death.

When I was twenty-six or twenty-seven and still in the midst of my drinking lifestyle, I went to a family gathering at my uncle John's condo. After drinking too much, I went up to his room to lie down. Hours passed, all the guests had left, and my uncle came up for the evening. I'm not proud to tell you that we both willingly engaged in a sexual encounter.

The next day, he had planned a business trip to a nearby state and asked me to join him for companionship during the journey. I agreed, and we were off on an adventure, stopping in pubs to drink and play pool, sharing laughter and intimacy.

Once the road trip came to an end, so did our forbidden relationship. For many years, I carried the guilt and shame of those few days and nights spent with my uncle. Eventually I got sober and began to grow up emotionally. My uncle passed away a few years later.

Late one night, I was driving home after attending one of my AA meetings, and suddenly the scent of cigar smoke filled my senses and lingered in the car. I was very aware that it was not my imagination, but in fact the presence of Uncle John. I was never so sure about anything. Then I clearly heard my uncle's voice say, "I am so sorry. I am so sorry."

I pulled over to the side of the road and began sobbing uncontrollably. Eventually I was filled with the most loving feelings from him and felt the need to say out loud, "I forgive you." A sense of deep calm and understanding came over me. It was a feeling of great love and care from my uncle—with a message that he would always watch over me to guide and protect me. I was so grateful to be in a receptive state for this experience of forgiveness to unfold. It was such a healing gift. Never again did I experience any regret or ill feelings about my uncle.

Sharon Reese's Story

Eight years ago while I was at work, I received an unexpected call from my sister-in-law. I can still remember the sound of her voice choking out three words that changed our lives, "Kyle's been killed."

My beautiful seventeen-year-old nephew, just beginning his senior year, had been coming down the mountain on his way to school when he hit a deer. He had crashed into a boulder and landed in a ravine. He died instantly. When I heard the news, I began screaming, "Oh my God!" over and over. I was incredibly distraught and grief-stricken.

A few hours later, our extended family gathered at my parents' house to grieve together. I was the first one to arrive. Still sobbing, I got out of my car, and something stopped me in my tracks.

As I stood there, Kyle "materialized" before me as if by magic. He completely took form. It was like something out of a science fiction movie. He appeared wet with light and had a bright yellow and green light glowing around him. He was smiling so big and seemed to be telepathically communicating with me. It was as if time had frozen still. I have no idea how long I stood there watching, maybe only a minute. Then something snapped me back and Kyle was gone.

In shock and disbelief, I opened the door and went into the house—only I felt completely different now. Instead of being an emotional wreck, I had a sense of peace and calm inside me. I began preparing food for the family. But I felt like a different person inside. I knew for sure that his visit was real and not just in my imagination. I'm not sure how or why I was able to see Kyle, but I do know that his visit eased my pain and was a special gift to me.

Part 2

Connecting with Your Departed Loved Ones

Chapter Four

Using Intuition to See the Other Side

It's 1980, and I'm home taking care of my thirty-four-year-old husband. His colon cancer was diagnosed one year ago. The journey has brought us here—far from where we dreamt our lives would take us. An antique iron bed we got as a wedding gift stands center stage in our tiny downstairs living room. Bags of IV fluid hang from the headboard, and a nasogastric tube and its empty canister sit on the dining table nearby. Paul refuses to use the NG tube to drain his stomach anymore—even though his intestines have completely shut down. Instead, he throws up bile every hour. He prefers that to using the tube.

On this warm July night, he stares wearily outside the window at the foothills that line the backyard of our apartment. Once these foothills were where we hiked and laughed together. Now, as we sit in bed holding hands, we both know this struggle can't go on much longer. He's made it clear that he wants to die at home, in my arms.

I fall asleep beside him for what feels like only ten minutes, when he wakens me. "I think you have to call Gwen," he says. I struggle to wake up and understand the new crisis. Gwen is our hospice nurse and comes to our house whenever we need her.

"What? What's going on?"

"I'm throwing up blood. Call Gwen. She'll know what to do," he says gently. I call Gwen. "I'll be there in a minute," she says, even though it's 2 a.m. True to her word, she's knocking on our front door in ten minutes.

Gwen bustles into action, taking vital signs, feeling Paul's stomach, and making phone calls. Within minutes, an ambulance is at our door. I'm too tired to fight it, even though it seems it will ruin his plan—to die at home. I crawl into the back of the ambulance and sit beside Paul on the stretcher. As we pull away from our apartment, Paul looks out the window at his shiny red BMW motorcycle parked in front of our apartment. This motorcycle has been his pride and joy—making him feel alive, healthy, and free this past year even when he wasn't.

As we pull away, he raises his hand and waves. "Bye, motorcycle." I know then that it's over. Our crazy struggle for a cure, a drug, a surgery, or a supplement that would give us our miracle is finished. We've lost the battle. As he weakly waves good-bye to his motorcycle, I say good-bye to the future we'll never share.

When they take him into the emergency room, Gwen goes with him. She asks me to stay in the waiting room. I know she's worried about me—looking so thin and tired. But this is my job, to take care of Paul. So I argue with her. She wins. I sit in the waiting room and fall asleep. In my dream, I see Paul hovering on the ceiling, looking down at a body on a table. I awake terrified.

Gwen comes to tell me they've stopped the bleeding and they're wheeling him into a hospital room upstairs. "He said he wanted to die at home," I insist. "This isn't what he wanted."

Gwen whispers calmly, "It's okay. I'm with you. It will be the way he wants it."

A wise doctor I've never met before arrives in our room and sits on Paul's bed. "Trust me. This will be okay," he says. "I've seen how these things go, and the process of dying takes its own course."

I'm exhausted, so I get in bed beside Paul. He holds me. "It's okay," he says. "When I was in the ER and they were putting a tube down my throat, I left my body. I was hovering on the ceiling, watching. I wasn't in any pain. You have to trust me. It's time to let go. I want you to give me a morphine overdose like you promised you would."

The wise doctor speaks up quickly: "Paul, listen. You can't ask Sue to do that. There's an easier way. You're so weak now that if we continue your prescribed dosage of morphine, it will build up in your system and you'll go to sleep. It'll be peaceful."

I'm not sure of anything anymore, so I stay quiet. Paul and the doctor discuss it. The morphine continues at the prescribed dosage.

Gwen disappears. Later I learn that she's called all our friends and family. By 6 a.m. our room is filled with loved ones, spilling out into the hallway. Paul's mother from Oklahoma is magically beside us, as well as my dear friend Betty from Missouri.

Betty and I walk the hospital hallways. I feel extraordinarily nauseated and am having some sort of anxiety attack. There's nothing in my stomach, so I retch dry heaves. Betty takes me outside to sit in the grass.

Betty, a natural healer and a physical therapist, holds my hand and talks me through my feelings. My anxiety is caused by guilt. I'm feeling guilty that Paul isn't having the kind of peaceful home death he wanted. I've let him down. Betty is logical and precise and explains calmly that this way is better, and that I haven't let him down. "You've done your best, and this is now the way it wants to go," she says.

As she says this, I realize that Paul's death is *my* letting go. Paul has already surrendered to the angels—left his body in the ER— and now is back to help me release him. It's me who needs to surrender. I realize this is the reason for my nausea; I need to let it all go. Almost as soon as I get this, my stomach feels better. We return to Paul's hospital room.

Paul calls me to his bedside. His voice is weak, but he's clear and precise. "I don't want you to waste your life grieving over me. I want you to get married and have babies. I'll always love you, but you must stay here and live your life. There are important things for you to do still," he says firmly. "Now get Bill. I want to talk to Bill."

Paul's best friend, Bill, an extraordinary mountaineer, sits on the bed. "I want you and Sue to take my ashes to the highest lake in North America," he whispers to Bill.

"I know exactly where that is," Bill says, smiling at his old friend with whom he's climbed numerous fourteen-thousand-foot peaks in the Rocky Mountains. Bill knows the lake is just outside of Breckenridge, where he and Paul have hiked before. This last request from Paul seems a bit strange and daunting.

"We'll do it, my friend," says Bill. "It'll be beautiful there this time of year." Other friends and family members are called to Paul's bedside for heartfelt farewells. Paul is clear and powerful in each of these final conversations. But after a while, he begins to drift in and out of consciousness.

Just before he slips into a coma, he calls me over to him one last time. He grabs a piece of paper and a pencil from the hospital tray. He writes in a scribbled hand, *Gifted.*

He hands me the paper. He can no longer speak. So he points to the word "gifted" and then to me with such power and presence, it takes my breath away. I have no idea what he means. Then his eyes close and his mouth opens and he slips deep into a coma, his breathing labored. It's hard to listen to.

Hours pass with Paul in this coma, breathing heavily, friends sitting on the floor around his bed and along the hallways, talking softly and sharing memories. In the corner, Paul's mother prays. I fall asleep on the floor beside the bed.

Instantly Paul appears in front of me—clear as day—looking young and healthy. "What are you waiting for?" he whispers clearly into my ear. "You said I could die in your arms. Get up and come hold me." He reaches down to get me. As his hand touches mine, I wake up.

The dream is so clear and his voice and presence so real that I'm startled awake—not sure where I am. I get to my feet and look around the room at the dozens of friends and family spilling out into the hall. I realize what I need to do and quickly ask everyone to leave the room except Paul's mother.

It's afternoon now, with a gentle rain falling outside the window. We can see the foothills vivid green through the summer shower. I stand on one side of Paul with my arms around him, and Ernie, his mom, stands on the other—rubbing his legs. His mother tells him she loves him and releases him to God. She prays. I rub his arms and chest.

"It's okay for you to go now, Paul," I whisper to him. "We love you and release you. I'll be fine. Your mom will be fine. Go play in the beautiful summer rain shower. You're free."

As soon as I finish speaking, after ten hours of loud and labored breathing, Paul takes one long, peaceful sigh. As he exhales this final breath, a filmy light vaporous being floats out of his body and slips gracefully across the room and out the window— disappearing into the gentle July rain.

I look at his mother. She's smiling and crying. "Did you see that?" I ask her. "Yes, yes . . . ," she says. We both look at his body on the bed. I know in every cell of my being that Paul no longer lives in that body. It's an empty shell, abandoned. I feel no attachment to it at all. Ernie and I walk to the window and look out. "He's free now," she whispers. "He's free."

I look out the window and my eyes go immediately to the foothills in the distance. I can sense Paul's joy around me, filling me with a calm happiness. His mother and I start laughing and crying, holding each other.

We walk into the hallway. "He's gone," I say, smiling. "It was beautiful, absolutely beautiful." I feel strangely elated. His friends begin crying with grief. Ernie and I comfort them, telling them it was peaceful and that he's free now.

I feel blessed to have witnessed his spirit leave his body. That final moment fuels the direction for the rest of my life. . . .

I'm working with a client, talking to her about her soul's mission. She's a teacher and works with children with disabilities. As a wise and intuitive Pisces 9-path soul, she needs to make a difference in the world. But her work has worn her out and she's going through a major reinvention. She wants to start a nonprofit foundation, work with adults, and write a book. She's feeling stuck and afraid.

As we talk, I get a brief glimpse of a large male standing to my right. His face is tough looking—makes me think of a bulldog. But he's begging for forgiveness. He's huge and intimidating, but his energy is meek and apologetic. I mention this to my client. "That's my father," she says slowly. "What's he saying?"

"He's saying he's sorry, very sorry," I tell her.

"Wow . . . He never said that when he was alive."

She tells me a story of years of childhood sexual abuse. She says he was a powerful man and she always feared him. She never confronted him and has never been able to forgive herself for allowing the abuse to continue for so many years.

The man to my right is practically yelling and crying. He's saying, "She didn't do anything wrong. It was all my fault. I see things so differently. She's an angel and always was. Tell her I'm so sorry. Tell her not to be afraid. What she wants in her future is going to happen."

As we talk, I help her see that her lesson is to forgive herself, realize her own power, and use her pain to move forward doing her great work. For so long she has believed her father was all-powerful, and yet still blamed herself for the abuse. These complicated feelings created enormous self-doubt and cynicism in her heart. Now maybe she can see him as a lost soul begging for forgiveness.

Our conversation helps her shift perspective. She agrees that her pain has made her a powerful teacher and writer. She will start a nonprofit and write her story of abuse and forgiveness. Realizing that she's the wise old soul and is her father's greatest teacher softens her pain. She takes a baby step forward by signing up for a class on nonprofit foundations.

In a dream, I'm walking through a beautiful space with tall windows from floor to ceiling. There are no square corners anywhere, and every room flows gracefully into the next. A metal spiral staircase leads to a bedroom with a stunning mountain view. A young boy is at my side, walking through the apartment with me. I tell him that I love the openness and want to live there.

I wake up from the dream still feeling the happiness of being in that space. My logical mind tells me that I had the dream because today I have to find a new apartment.

It's 1980, and my husband has just died. I've moved out of our home and am staying with friends while I look for a new place to live. I'm exhausted and overwhelmed, going through newspaper ads, trying to find something I can afford that won't be too small or depressing. I call and make appointments to visit five apartments that day.

As I drive toward my first appointment, I see a rental sign in the driveway of an unusual-looking complex. A voice inside me says, "Pull in there now." It's not logical, and I have other appointments that I'm already late for. Yet I pull into the driveway.

A sign leads me to the manager's apartment. A boy around twelve years old tells me through the door that his mother won't be home from work until five, and that she handles the rentals. I tell him that I just want to look at it. Could he give me the key if I give him my driver's license as a deposit for the key?

He opens the door and says he'll show me the place. He's the boy in my dream. I'm getting goose bumps and my heart rate is accelerating as he opens the door to the apartment. I follow him in and see the exact space I just dreamed about—down to the unusual angles, tall windows, spiral staircase, upstairs bedroom with the view. I start laughing and telling him, "This is my home. I dreamed about this place. This is where I'm supposed to live. . . ."

After he shows me the apartment, he tells me that I still have to wait until his mom gets home at five, and that she's got other people with appointments to see it. I tell him that I can give him a check for the deposit and the first month's rent. Maybe he could call his mom and tell her I want it.

He's pretty savvy and tells me I have to wait.

I spend the entire day waiting outside his front door. (Poor kid.) I realize that I've blown off all the other appointments I had, and that if this one doesn't work out, I won't have a place to live.

But my gut is saying that this is my home and that I dreamt of it exactly as it is, so it's meant to be. During the day, several others show up, wanting to see the space. But I tell everyone that I'm going to take the apartment and am waiting with the check for the manager to come home. I don't budge. At one point, five of us stand outside the boy's door, negotiating.

When the woman finally comes home, against all the odds, she says yes to me and takes my check. (She tells me months later that she had a "gut feeling" that I was the right person to live there.) It's been a day of trusting my dream, trusting my gut, and finding the home that I would live in for many years to come. It was a sacred healing space for me, and I know that Paul found it for me, revealed it to me in a dream, and drove my car into the driveway to see it. I'm forever grateful.

What Is Intuition?

Yes, we're *all* intuitive and naturally able to access our right brains—which embody our intuition, creativity, and connection to divinity. Yet we talk ourselves out of listening to this inner guidance by focusing on our left-brain chatter—which is our linear, practical, realistic mind. Meditation quiets this monkey mind so we can better tune into our intuition and our higher self. Accessing intuition allows us to communicate powerfully with our departed and follow our inner guidance.

Yet many people are so firmly rooted in this physical world that they believe *only* what they can see with their eyes is real. However, our sense of sight is complex and gives us much more information from the other realms than our minds can efficiently process. The glimmer of a spirit in the corner of the room has no logical purpose for our daily survival. It distracts us from getting the laundry done. So the logical left brain filters out this information; it has learned from years of societal conditioning what is real and unreal. The conditioned mind determines that the spirit in the corner is not crucial for survival and filters it out.

This mental processing is what causes our limited beliefs about the true nature of our reality. This reality filter, graciously provided by the linear mind to ensure survival, prevents us from understanding who we really are and how this multidimensional world works.

When we close our eyes, we quiet much of this logical left-brain chatter. We begin to *feel* through our other senses—including our sixth sense—the intuitive connection to the divine.

When we lose a loved one, our logical mind tells us that they've left us. So we feel alone and abandoned. Yet by simply closing our eyes, repeating prayer or mantra, and speaking directly to the departed, we can feel their presence. The other realms are as close to us as the clothes that we're wearing are to our skin. Yet this is hard for us to comprehend because our eyes don't translate that information to us.

Sensing our departed standing beside us is not a matter of seeing a perfectly formed being. Our departed will rarely materialize fully for us—unless there's an emergency or something essential they need to say with no other way of getting our attention. This kind of complete materialization is rare and difficult for a spirit in the higher realms to achieve (although it does happen). Complete materialization requires enormous energy from the departed.

Their daily visits to us appear more as fleeting glimpses, or hazy images in the corner of our vision—not directly in front of us. Our eyes may be scanning a room when we catch something in our field of vision that resembles a human form. But when we turn to look directly at it, the image is often no longer there because we've activated our left-brain reality filter.

We sense a presence when a departed loved one is near. We may see an image in our mind's eye, get goose bumps, hear a whisper, or even smell a familiar scent.

Yet when we're lost in grief, our sadness and depression create a gray energy cloud, which blocks our ability to sense their presence and prevents them from communicating directly with us.

Drugs and alcohol also cloud our energy field and disrupt communication with the other realms. They lower our vibrational frequency. When you're grieving, a healthy and clean lifestyle raises your frequency and enhances your ability to connect to the divine and to your departed.

Sitting in prayer or meditation for twenty minutes each morning, you can raise your frequency, release your pain, and clear your channel to the divine. This daily practice requires discipline—but the benefits are enormous.

Daily mantra-based meditation opens you up to your right brain, which is where your higher consciousness lives. From there, you have easy access to information from your guides and departed loved ones, as well as your higher self.

I've described my Break Your Heart Wide Open Meditation in the following chapter. To briefly summarize: Sit in prayer or meditation with eyes closed for twenty minutes. Then ask to feel the full heartbreak of your loss. Allow yourself to cry the pain out. Offer your pain to the divine beings to carry away and transform into love. Then speak directly to your departed. Ask for their guidance. Tell them how much you love them. Ask for strength to carry on and accomplish your great work. Because they have a soul mate agreement with you, they will assist you in moving forward—especially when you ask them to.

Take note throughout the day of when you experience a sense of knowingness about a difficult situation, have a feeling of peace wash over you from nowhere, or bump into an old friend who makes you laugh and feel better. Your loved one is helping you in these moments.

Through practice, you'll learn to trust the information you get from your higher self and use it in your daily life.

At the end of your day, sit again in quiet prayer or meditation with eyes closed. After twenty minutes, feel and release the pain in your heart. Offer it up to the universe to be transmuted into love and gratitude. Speak directly to your loved ones and thank them for the gifts they've put in your path that day. Tell them you realize they're watching over you and that you're grateful.

Trusting Your Right Brain

You *do* have a powerful right brain, and you've had many intuitive experiences during your life, although you may have dismissed them as nonsense. Do you remember knowing when something was true, or seeing a brief glimpse into your future, or having a dream that gave you insight into a problem? Did you trust the information you received? What did you learn from these intuitive experiences?

Remember the last time you fell in love—the moment your hand first brushed the hand of someone who would later become your greatest partner? Do you remember when you knew you were pregnant before the test confirmed it? Do you remember feeling intuitively connected to your departed loved one before he died?

Most of us trust our intuition when it pertains to love— whether it's the love of a partner or a child. However when we lose a loved one, pain shuts down this intuitive pathway simply because pain shuts down the heart.

Your heart is the gateway to your intuition. The more you cling to your thoughts, the harder it is to open your heart and feel the truth. Meditation quiets your mind and helps you trust your heart. It will strengthen your intuitive connection to the other realms.

Here are some techniques to strengthen your intuition:

Right now, test out a possible choice in your future to see how it feels in your body. This could be a small choice, such as what restaurant to go to or a large choice such as what business to start or job to take.

See yourself doing this as if it's already been decided and you're living in that future, conducting the details of your future day-to- day life. Notice everything around you. How does this new life feel?

Check in with your physical body. Are you smiling and feeling good in this possible future? If so, that's a yes from your intuition. If you feel tired, drained, or fearful in your body, that's a no from your intuition.

Practice intuition every day. Before heading home from work ask: "Should I take this route or the other?" Then close your eyes and see yourself on one of the possible routes and note how your body feels. Do you get a good or bad feeling in response to seeing that particular drive? If it's good, take that route home.

Afterwards, reflect on how the commute went for you. Was it easier than usual? Was there less traffic?

Plan an intuitively guided vacation. Visit a new city and choose activities for the day based on your gut feelings. Keep a journal of how this works for you.

As you learn to trust your intuition for these little everyday choices, you'll be better able to trust your intuition for the big life choices of love, career, and health. *And* you'll finally trust your intuitive connection to your departed loved ones. This will truly heal your loss.

You can also get dream guidance from your departed whenever you need it. Before going to sleep, ask your departed to communicate directly with you in your dreams in a way that you can remember in the morning. Or ask specifically for a healing dream. In the morning, sit up in bed and write down images or feelings you remember.

Then repeat the Break Your Heart Wide Open Meditation. Beginning and ending each day in divine connection with the other realms will speed your recovery and fill your life with grace. It also benefits your loved ones on the other side. They're finally able to help you.

Your Daily Reconnection Ritual
The most powerful way to explain how intuition works is to teach you my Daily Reconnection Ritual. This technique is so simple, and anyone can do it. It works whether your loved one just crossed over or crossed over decades ago.

I began doing this right after my husband, Paul, died and it was very powerful. But I put it aside, telling myself that he had moved on to other lifetimes and I shouldn't bother him. That decision left me feeling extraordinarily lonely, and it wasn't true that Paul had moved on and was inaccessible to me. He was trying to help me move forward.

Time is not linear and doesn't move from point A to point B in the way that we think of it here. The quantum physicists teach that time and space are happening at once. We can access all the realms and travel through time and space once we release our limited view of how things work. For me, this meant embracing a bigger picture and understanding that Paul had moved on—but was also available to me for guidance. Since then, I've found his guidance profoundly helpful in my life—whether I was asking if my daughter would get into a good college or needed help writing a section of my book.

Your loved ones are always there for you. Please suspend whatever limited thinking is holding you back from reconnecting with your departed. You'll be amazed at the powerful guidance and loving energy you receive when you reach out. Here's how it works:

1. **Sit in a quiet space and close your eyes.** If it's noisy, use earplugs to create quiet. Take three deep breaths.

2. **Repeat a high-frequency Sanskrit phrase like *Om Namah Shivaya*** ("I bow to the divine self") or **repeat the Lord's Prayer.** You can do this quietly in your head. When you notice your thoughts getting in the way, gently bring your focus back to the mantra. I recommend either using this mantra or the Lord's Prayer. You're trying to raise your energy frequency and don't want to attract lost souls. Sanskrit mantras and the Lord's Prayer carry sacred energy and will protect you.

3. At the end of fifteen minutes (when you've noticed your mind settling down), stop repeating the mantra and keep your eyes closed. Take a deep breath and open your heart. **Send loving energy to your departed.** Feel the love and see them feeling it and smiling back at you. Love protects you from anything negative and strengthens your intuition. It opens your connection to the departed.

4. **Speak directly to your loved one.** Say, "Hi . . . are you there?" With your eyes closed, notice the flicker of an image in front of you. Don't fixate on the image or look directly at it. Keep your eyes closed. But be aware that your loved one is taking form for you. Don't be afraid. Concentrate on feeling love in your heart. It enhances your connection and protects you.

5. **Ask your most pressing questions.** Examples: Will you help me write my book? Can you help me find love and companionship? What should I do for a living? Can you help me feel stronger? Why am I still here? Why did you have to go? What should I do now?

6. **Be quiet and listen.** They're speaking to you. You may doubt it because it will feel as if you're imagining the conversation. You're not.

This is how they communicate. If you're feeling cynical, tell yourself, "Okay this is a fun game of imagination. . . ." But stick with it. Take note of everything they say, the ideas that pop into your head, and the images you get. This is all guidance for you.

7. **Send them gratitude!** Say: "Thank you for your help! I feel your presence and I appreciate it!"

8. **Write** down any ideas, phrases, images, or feelings you received or that come to you now upon reflection.

9. Get up and go about your day. Later take time to reflect on what you experienced. **Contemplate** how the guidance applies to your life.

Practice this Reconnection Ritual at least once a day. If at first you doubt the connection and talk yourself out of believing the images and whispers are real, ask your departed for a sign to help you believe. You can ask for flickering lights or a phone call with no one on the other end. Or you can ask to have someone say something to you that day that replicates a phrase you used with your departed.

If you practice this ritual once a day for seven days, it will remove any doubt that your loved one lives on and is still accessible to you. You'll gain a new perspective on your life and see why you're still here. Remember, you have to surrender what you "know" and quiet the logical mind to experience this powerful connection.

Once you begin daily meditation to access your higher consciousness, you also open yourself up to other energies. Just as there are positive energies in the universe, there are negative ones. Our universe is composed of both light and dark, yin and yang. When we venture into the other realms, we need to wrap ourselves in high-frequency prayer, mantra, or chanting for protection.

It's also important to ground yourself in basic spiritual principles before dabbling in the higher realms. Whenever you connect to your departed loved one, you're opening up to other dimensions.

Protection Techniques

The Lord's Prayer has been used in the Christian tradition for centuries to call in the light and protect us from dark energies. It's an extremely powerful high-vibration prayer. Repeat it whenever you feel afraid.

The mantra *Om Namah Shivaya* is a Sanskrit phrase meaning, "I bow to the divine self." This sacred, high-vibration chant has been used for thousands of years to raise consciousness and will also wrap you in protective energy. I use it every day in my meditations and before working with my clients.

Energy healers use techniques such as picturing a bubble of white or blue light surrounding and protecting them. I've also found this to be helpful.

In my years of studying Hinduism and Buddhism, I've used many spiritual cleansing techniques, but here is my favorite: Sit on the ground in meditation position with legs folded. Extend your arms straight down to the ground so that your fingertips touch the floor. Visualize running energy from the top of your head down through your fingertips and into the ground. This practice works to flush negativity and exhaustion from your body and sends them into the earth to be recycled.

Water is a powerful cleansing agent and you can use it to do more than cleanse your body. Swimming, showering, or taking a bath will also energetically cleanse you—washing away dark or negative energies and feelings you've picked up during the day. Adding salt to your bathwater gives it more energy-cleansing power. If water isn't available, sit in meditation and picture a shower or waterfall pouring over your head and washing everything away until you feel pure and light.

Love is the most powerful positive force of all and it always trumps darkness. When you're afraid, send love to what you fear. It's like turning on a light in a dark room. Open your heart and pump the love. Darkness will disappear.

When you're afraid, this technique will help you: Sit in meditation until you can feel love for just one person in your life. See that person wrapped in your powerful love. Pump the love to this person until you see them smiling and laughing. Now extend that love energy out to the entire space around you, filling it with golden light. Now pump your love out to the entire world. See our planet wrapped in golden love and light, and all of its people looking peaceful and happy. Spend time with that image. When you open your eyes, the room you're sitting in will shimmer with love and light. Your fear will be gone.

Chapter Five

YOUR DAILY HEALING AND RECONNECTION SCHEDULE

Follow this schedule for one month, and you'll feel revitalized and energized. Or use it when you're going through a rough patch to renew your spirit.

Recovering from grief is a day-by-day, one-foot-in-front-of-the- other process. If you're ready to start feeling better, this daily plan will get you there. Please give this routine at least three weeks—no matter how hard it may seem in the beginning. At the end of three weeks, you'll feel happier and more hopeful about your future. Your sadness will lighten, and your life force will strengthen. Put a stickie on this page of the book and refer to the schedule each day.

5 a.m.: Wake Up Early and Pray!

When the sun comes up, there's a surge of energy that allows you to reenter the physical realm feeling revitalized after journeying to the higher realms in your dreams. And it's been said that the angels begin praying each morning at 5 a.m. and that you can tap into their powerful healing energy if you join them. When you're grieving, sleeping past sunrise makes your waking-up process more emotionally painful. Set your alarm for no later than 6 a.m. or whenever the sun comes up in your area. Sit up and immediately do the Break Your Heart Wide Open Meditation.

The Break Your Heart Wide Open Meditation

This is a powerful way to release your grief and begin to heal. This practice will make you feel better from the first day you try it. I've used it many times in my life and it has helped hundreds of my grieving clients.

1. Start each morning with a ten- to twenty-minute meditation. During this meditation, quiet your mind with mantra or prayer repetition. I repeat the ancient mantra *Om Namah Shivaya*, a Sanskrit phrase meaning "I bow to the divine self." Or you can repeat the Lord's Prayer.

2. Whenever your thoughts wander into your meditation, gently bring your focus back to the mantra.

3. At the end of the meditation, when your mind has settled down, ask to fully feel and release the pain in your heart. Hold your open palm facing upward in front of your heart. Focus your attention on the heart, take several deep breaths, and allow yourself to experience your grief deeply. Cry if you need to.

4. Picture the pain moving from your heart and into your upward-facing palm. Move the palm out and away from you and then above toward God. Say, "I release this pain for my highest good and transform it into love." Imagine your tears carrying the pain away from you and up to the highest realms. Say, "Please, divine guides, take this pain from my heart and burn it up for me."

5. If you're ready to feel the presence of your departed loved one, say: "Good morning. I miss you. I love you." Ask: "Do you have any guidance for me?" Listen and write down any messages, feelings, or images you receive. You can say: "I feel angry, sad, and hurt that you left me and I need help releasing these feelings so I can move on. Please help me."

6. Repeat this meditation again at the end of the day before going to sleep. By starting and ending each day with this process, your grief will soon dissolve, and you'll find the energy to move forward with your life.

6 a.m.: Move Your Chi

Waking up to meditate and then exercise will prime your *chi,* or "life force," in such a way that your grief will soon feel lighter. Studies show that thirty minutes of daily exercise is more effective at curing depression than prescription medication. This potent combination of early morning meditation and exercise will open you up to experience joy again.

When my husband died, I signed up for a 5 a.m. exercise class a few blocks from my house at a local recreation center. It was so difficult to drag myself out of bed. (I wasn't sleeping well.) And I didn't manage it every morning. But when I did, I always returned home feeling exhilarated and ready to have a good day.

When you first experience loss, you may not even feel up to leaving the house. That's fine. Start at home. Buy an exercise DVD or find an exercise class on your local cable TV channel.

Wake up early, meditate, get out of bed, drink water, and do your thirty-minute exercise program. You can start with moderate exercise. Just get your four limbs moving—whether it's dancing, yoga, or tai chi.

You need to move your body to get the life force flowing again. Life force is the antidote to your grief and depression. Exercising first thing in the morning enhances your energy for the rest of the day. Physical movement starts your day with a boost of endorphins, the feel-good hormone. Exercising at the end of your day releases stress and helps you sleep better. But to start your day off right, meditate as soon as you awaken, followed immediately by thirty minutes of exercise.

When you begin to feel better, add thirty minutes of walking or running to your midday routine. You can do this on your lunch break. It raises your energy and helps you get through the afternoon.

Eventually you may want to join a group class or a fitness club. Exercising with a class will help you feel connected to others. Don't expect yourself to get to the gym five days a week. It just won't happen consistently. Life intervenes. Start with thirty minutes of exercise in your living room in front of your DVD. Going to the fitness club two or three times a week is a perfect addition to that, and will help you feel a sense of community.

7 a.m.: Feed Your Chi

Whenever we're in pain, we seem to be drawn to eat comfort foods like mac and cheese or sweets like ice cream. We think those foods will make us feel better. But they really only drain our energy. When we're grieving, we need to treat our bodies as if we're recovering from a physical illness. Indeed, you *have* been physically traumatized by your loss, and eating unhealthy comfort food now will only deplete you and make you feel worse.

Healing grief requires boosting your immune system and enhancing your life force. I recommend a two-week raw foods diet to cleanse your system and recharge your health. You can learn more about this diet in many books, such as *Rawsome,* by Brigitte Mars (Basic Health Publications, 2004), a well-known herbalist, author, and raw foods proponent. (Visit Brigitte's Web site, www.BrigitteMars.com, for more information.)

The raw foods diet is so packed with nutrients that you'll feel energized within the first few days of eating raw. Meet with a raw foods consultant to help plan your meals so that you get enough protein and B vitamins. Uncooked foods carry a powerful life force, and you need plenty of life force now. Nibbling raw fruit, vegetables, and nuts throughout the day will energize you. Eating chips and sweet snacks all day will drain you and lower your immune system. Keep in mind that eating processed foods and sugar has been shown to deplete your body of B vitamins, which are essential to emotional health.

In fact, depletion of B vitamins has been linked to depression and schizophrenia. Take a good B-vitamin daily supplement. And ask your local natural foods retailer to suggest a Saint-John's-wort herbal supplement; it's been shown in research to ease depression. Bach flower remedies (such as Rescue Remedy and Beech) are also used to improve mood and reduce the effects of emotional trauma. Rose and lemon essential oils are used to heal the heart and uplift the spirit. The homeopathic remedy ignatia is beneficial for reducing sadness and healing grief. All these remedies can be found in your local natural foods store.

Noon: Have a Chat with Your Departed

In your morning meditation, explain to your departed that you'd like to check in with them again at noon and later at 6 p.m. This helps you release your need to think about them throughout the day—knowing that you'll connect at a later time.

To connect at the appointed time, do the Reconnection Ritual. Or just say, "Hey, I'm checking in to say hello. Do you have any guidance for me? What should I do about such and such? . . ."

Listen for their end of the conversation. Write down any ideas or insights that come to you. Do this again around dinnertime or 6 p.m.

After a few months of doing this, you'll feel less of a need for daily connection with your departed. You'll simply know it's time to let go, and that will feel okay with you. You'll know that whenever you need to talk, your loved one will find you.

You may think that your loved one has moved on to the higher realms or has incarnated back into this realm. This is not your concern. Time and space are not linear, and we have a very limited understanding of how time works. The quantum physicists say that time and space are all happening at once. Your loved one can be in a higher realm or even another lifetime and still connect with you here and now.

If your departed left you years ago, and you've suddenly hit a wave of grief, this is probably because of a new loss occurring in your life, such as the end of a relationship or the loss of a job. Use this opportunity to reconnect with your departed and get fresh guidance for this reinvention point in your life.

2 p.m. Midafternoon Energy Boost

We usually hit an energy slump around midafternoon. This is when we're most tempted to eat sweets for a quick boost. But a sugar high will cause a painful energy crash later on. Instead, try something different. How about doing afternoon energy experiments to raise your vibration level and promote well-being in your life.

Instead of a snack, practice wild forgiveness and random gratitude toward office mates or people you interact with. Tell a coworker something about herself that you're grateful for. Walk up to someone with whom you've experienced negative energy in the past, and send fearless love and forgiveness their way. Look them in the eye and tell them something wonderful and true about themselves. Call a family member with whom you've had a strained relationship. Tell them how awesome they are and wrap them in forgiveness.

Feeling gratitude and forgiveness toward others will enhance your own energy and feed your soul. It will take the focus away from your pain and open your heart, which is essential for healing.

6 p.m.: Evening Meditation to Release Grief

Around 6 p.m., or whenever the sun sets, there's another energy shift that you can use to tap into the energy of prayer and connect to your departed.

Find a quiet space to sit in meditation. Close your eyes and repeat *Om Namah Shivaya* or the Lord's Prayer. Repeat those sacred words/sounds for ten to twenty minutes without getting up or opening your eyes.

When you notice your mind wandering, gently bring your focus back to the words you're repeating.

Hold your open palm facing upward in front of your heart chakra. Ask to feel your sadness. Experience it in your body. If you're able to cry, release the pain through your tears.

With the palm facing upward, imagine placing your pain and sadness into your hand. Move the palm out and away from you and then toward God.

Say, "I release this pain for my highest good and for all those who suffer."

Then say, "Thank you for helping me today. I'm open to any guidance."

Write down any ideas or insights that come to you. Then get up and go about your evening routine.

Eat a healthy dinner with as few processed foods as possible. Think of yourself as having been injured and needing to nurse your body back to health. Stay away from caffeine or alcohol— especially in the evening, when you may be tempted to have wine with dinner. Though a glass of wine may feel good at the moment, in the long run it weakens your connection to the higher realms. Even one glass of wine clouds your energy, lowers your vibration, and makes you more prone to depression.

10 p.m.: Prepare for Sleep by Reconnecting Again to Your Loved One
Before going to sleep, say prayers or do your evening meditation. Close your eyes and repeat *Om Namah Shivaya* or the Lord's Prayer for ten to twenty minutes without getting up or opening your eyes.

When you notice your mind wandering, gently bring your focus back to the words you're repeating. Say, "Please, divine guides, take this pain from my heart and burn it up for me."

When you're ready to feel the presence of your departed loved one, say: "Thank you. I felt you with me today. I'd be grateful if you could help me heal while I sleep."

Chapter Six

QUESTIONS FROM READERS
ABOUT THEIR DEPARTED

During my workshops and sessions, I'm often asked thought- provoking questions from people who've lost a loved one. The answers I've written here have helped quite a few people. I wanted to share them with you.

Q: *How can we tell for sure they're still with us in some way? I hope, but I don't really know.*

A: Your loved one *is* trying to communicate with you. But your logical mind (left brain) dismisses these messages as meaningless or coincidental. To experience this communication directly with your departed, you have to quiet your monkey mind. Sitting in silent daily meditation will open up your right-brain expanded consciousness and make you receptive to these messages. The more you meditate, the more you'll experience the connection; you'll be able to hear clear communications from your loved ones. Try this: After you've sat quietly in meditation for twenty minutes, place your hand over your heart chakra and take a deep breath. As you breathe in, feel the love you have for your departed loved one. The love you feel will draw them near you. When you feel their presence, ask a direct question. Open your mind and listen. Don't dismiss what you hear as imagination. It's not. Learn to trust your intuition and write down the impressions you get.

Q: *How do we know they're still here and connecting with us? After my grandmother died, the phone would ring (with no one on the other end) every time we talked about her. We still talk about her twenty-five years later, but the phone doesn't ring.*

A: She has moved on to a higher realm, as she should for her soul's evolution. But you do still have access to her when you directly request her presence through prayer or meditation. And because your grief isn't quite so strong now as when you first lost her, you can't call her into this realm simply by talking about her. Next time you're thinking of her, open your heart and feel the love you hold for her. Feel it and marinate in it. Then ask her a direct question, and you'll get an answer.

Q: *How do I let go and release the yearning for the physical presence? I miss hearing my daughter's voice, smelling her hair, and seeing her face.*

A: Yearning for the physical presence of a departed loved one is the greatest pain we can experience. This is what makes grieving for a child especially painful—you miss the sweet feel of the physical body. And if you've lost your spouse, you'll miss the passionate connection you once shared. We must surrender this need for the physical form when someone crosses over. It only increases our pain and prevents us from moving forward. Our departed are no longer in a physical form, and we can experience them more profoundly now by connecting to them intuitively. Practice the Break Your Heart Wide Open Meditation. After you've released some of your pain by practicing this technique, ask to feel your loved one's presence through transmitted thoughts, voices, or visions. Ask them to comfort you this way whenever possible. It's also helpful to engage in daily physical exercise such as walking, running, dance, or yoga. This activity stimulates your life force, so that you're not stuck in the stagnation of longing.

Q: *Do their spirits watch us every day? And if so, do they know everything that we do—even when we do something that's not good? Do they judge us as they did while they were here on earth since now they're at a different level of awareness?*

A: Their guides in the higher realms keep them busy with study and learning so they don't just hang around, watching us. But they're drawn to us when we feel strong emotions such as grief, fear, and love. So if you're feeling great fear, they'll be beside you. When you feel the enormous love you have for them, they'll be beside you. And, yes, they have a very different view of things once they cross over and experience their life review. An action that you might think is terribly bad, they will see as an experience you've chosen to learn from.

Q: *Why did my departed loved one go through so much physical suffering at the end of his life?*

A: Often a highly evolved soul will choose to go through physical suffering at the end of life as a way to quickly burn up any negativity they may have carried with them through past lifetimes. They're trying to break negative patterns that they've been unable to break in other ways. Physical suffering can purify our souls of negativity—if we let it. After a year of terrible suffering, my husband, Paul, became a radiant shining light being with only love and compassion in his heart. The experience of dying a painful death was similar for Crissie and my father. I believe my father, who had been raised Catholic, believed he was unworthy of heaven and used his final days of suffering to cleanse his soul and purify his heart. By the time he crossed over, he was gloriously at peace. We *don't* have to choose physical suffering to evolve our souls. There are many other ways. But those who do choose it are determined to break the cycle of reincarnation and experience oneness with God. As I've mentioned before, being here in this physical realm is a great challenge to us energetically and spiritually. Once we cross over, we return to the blissful realms and usually have little desire to come back. Those of us left here, who cared for our dying loved ones, are also trying to further our soul's growth. But to learn the lesson offered and evolve, we must move beyond the pain.

Q: *Why do we have to die?*

A: From where we stand in this physical realm, we really don't understand who we are or we wouldn't ask that question. The word "death" is so misleading. Nothing dies except our physical body—which is a mere shell, or a costume, that we chose for this brief stint in the physical world. We're energy beings, souls on a journey who briefly dropped into this physical world for an evolutionary experience. We chose to come here to help raise consciousness. If we could change the word from "die" to "evolve," then we would take away the negative energy around our natural return to the realms we came from. This lifetime is only a brief blip in the soul's journey. We think of death as tragic only because we miss our loved ones. Yet from their perspective, they haven't left us. They're waiting for us to fulfill our soul mission so we can join them. They've graduated! We should be celebrating!

Q: *The car accident that killed my husband was a random tragedy; I know he wasn't ready to cross over. . . .*

A: In spite of how it looks to you, our souls *do* choose our exact final breath here and the exact method of leaving the body. It's all outlined in the soul map that we cocreated with divine guidance before dropping in for this lifetime. If your loved one was killed in a drunk-driving accident caused by another driver, your loved one had a karmic soul agreement with that driver and with you. You all agreed to experience this tragedy to help catapult all of you into the next level of your evolution as a soul group. This tragedy is your opportunity to evolve to a higher level of consciousness. As long as you hold on to blame and anger about the accident, you're not fulfilling your agreement with your departed loved one. It hurts them to see you wallow in painful, negative emotions. They want to see you move forward and accomplish your great work so that you can join them in the highest realms.

Q: *How can there be a God if my brother died so randomly in a boating accident?*

A: This question is really about your definition of God. Do you believe that God is a man in the sky who punishes you for your sins and allows your loved ones to die randomly in boating accidents? Or do you believe that you're a divine being who came here on purpose with a plan, and that God is the light source from which you emerged and into which you'll return? I'm asking you to consider a much bigger view of spirituality and understand that everything is on purpose and exactly as you planned it before coming here. You and your brother signed up for this event for your highest good. Please go on a spiritual exploration journey and study the theologies of all great religions from Christianity to Buddhism, Hinduism, and Judaism—as well as metaphysics and quantum physics. Sooner or later, you'll understand the common thread of spiritual truth that runs through all paths. As you learn to meditate and quiet your monkey mind, you'll feel a connection to something greater than yourself. This will eventually bring you to an understanding of divine order. You'll see that nothing is a tragedy—and that everything is lined up perfectly for your highest good.

Q: *How do I help my young children understand where their mommy went?*

A: Very young children are naturally intuitive and still connected to the divine realms. It's not hard for them to understand that their loved one has moved on to these other realms and will be their guardian angel protecting them. This makes sense to them because they haven't yet completely disengaged from their higher consciousness. They can still see the other realms and will probably report to you that they've seen their mommy. It's important that when this happens you don't deny that their mom is still with them. She'll always watch over them. This is your chance to embrace your highest self and bring a spiritual perspective into your daily life. It may require a spiritual reawakening. Your children can lead the way. Become a strong role model for living a spiritually aware life, and you'll help your children tremendously. I'm not talking about religion. I'm talking about spirituality, which is a much broader understanding of who we are as divine beings and why we're here. If you're not clear on that, for your children's sake, it's time to figure it out. As long as your children have a sense of connection to something greater than the physical world and they know that you embrace this too, they will find their way through the pain. When a child is older, especially in the teen years, they have much more trouble understanding a parent's death. They've usually shut down or diminished their connection to higher consciousness and are more rooted in this mundane physical world. This loss presents a powerful opportunity for you to open them back up to their higher consciousness and embrace a spiritual perspective. Ask your teen to go on a meditation retreat weekend with you. Take her to hear speakers like Deepak Chopra or Michael Beckwith. Share movies that help open the mind to a world beyond the physical, such as *What the Bleep Do We Know!?* Talk to them honestly about your experiences and answer their questions fully. A highly evolved spiritual therapist can also help ease them through this painful time.

Q: *My spouse was randomly shot in a convenience store robbery just because he walked in at the wrong time. It wasn't his choice to die. I won't be at peace until the killer is convicted. Help me!*

A: If I could show you a glimpse of yourself from the viewpoint of the higher realms—where your spouse is—you would see how anger and revenge create a gray cloud around you. This dark energy (created by your negative emotions) prevents your departed spouse from communicating with you. It also poisons your heart and sends your life in the wrong direction. This dark cloud of energy you've created is not hurting your husband's killer, only you. When you begin to see your life as an intentional journey with every moment on purpose, you'll understand the uselessness of blame. It's like drinking poison and expecting the other person to die. You need to focus the fuel of your anger into positive steps for yourself—finding your great work and helping others. This will remove the gray cloud and open you up to experience the love and divine guidance you came here to know. Don't worry about needing to punish your husband's killer. Each of us has a soul review at the moment of crossing over. Your spouse's killer will experience a personal "hell" when they glimpse their actions through the spiritual perspective that accompanies the final life review. They'll be bound to spend further lifetimes reversing their negative actions and repaying karmic debts. It's not your job to be his judge. Focus on your own path and accomplish your soul mission so you can join your spouse in the highest realms.

Q: *My young daughter was kidnapped and murdered. I'm so angry at God and at the world. How do I move on?*

A: I'm sorry that you've had to live through this. But your anger and depression are not what your daughter wants to see you experiencing. If you can shift perspective, please consider that this painful death was a karma that you, your daughter, and her killer all chose to experience for each of your souls' highest evolution. If you could see the tiny blip this one lifetime represents in the long journey of your daughter's soul, you'd understand why you both chose this experience. Your daughter exited this lifetime exactly when she meant to—even if it seemed too soon for you. Her soul mission for this lifetime was fulfilled. Now she watches over you, hoping you'll fulfill your soul mission, do your great work, and help others. The more you linger in your pain, the more you prevent your own inevitable evolution. Embrace the lessons of forgiveness and compassion that you were meant to learn from this painful event. Your anger prevents your daughter's high-frequency energy from reaching out to you. She wants to comfort you, but your grief is like a wall that she can't reach through. If you knew she was watching, how would you live your life? What would you do next? Meditate and find your answers. Live your life as a monument to her soul instead of focusing only on how she exited this lifetime.

Q: *Since my daughter's death, I see no purpose in my life anymore. Why can't I cross over and be with her now?*

A: If you're still here taking another breath, it means your soul has determined it's not time for you to leave yet. You still have something important to do here. Your loved one waits just beyond your reach, hoping you'll remember your magnificent soul mission. Once you realize that your pain is the fuel for doing your great work, your next step will appear in front of you, beckoning like a light in the fog. Take a baby step toward fulfilling your purpose. Ask yourself, "What talents and gifts did I bring with me that could help the world? What's one step I could take now to investigate that new direction? How can I do this in a way that makes my daughter proud of me?" Do your great work, help others with the wisdom you've gained, and you'll soon be able to cross over and join her. When you've lost a young child, you may feel that she needs you to care for her. But your child is a spirit—not a body—and she's wrapped in love on the other side. She wants to help *you* now.

She's a fully evolved soul, not a physical baby who needs to be cared for. It's only in this realm that the human body needs to be cared for so intensely. The soul lives on and prospers in the other realms, surrounded by loved ones, guides, and angels. Know that if you choose suicide, you'll see things very differently when you cross over. Your soul review will reveal the other, more productive choices you could have made. You'll regret having gotten lost in negative energy. The pain that your suicide causes your loves ones will hurt you tremendously. You'll see its repercussions from the higher realms. Suicide makes future lifetimes more challenging as you work to reverse the pain and suffering you've caused others.

Q: *I've had two miscarriages and I'm grieving the loss of those two babies. I'm blaming myself for somehow causing the miscarriages (although the doctor says it wasn't my fault), and I'm afraid to try to get pregnant again. I feel sad nearly every day. Can you help me?*

A: You've done nothing wrong, and the spirits of your babies are alive and well and trying to comfort you. You were fulfilling a soul agreement with them. They're your greatest teachers and they love you very much. They were opening your heart to prepare you for the child who is coming next and will stay to live with you in the physical realms. Do you agree that your heart has been broken wide open by these losses? Do you agree that when you finally hold the baby in your arms who is coming to stay that you will love this baby in a profound and grateful way— especially because of the losses you've been through? This is the purpose of the agreement. Instead of wrapping yourself in sadness now—which won't allow the spirit of your next child to enter, wrap yourself in love and gratitude to prepare your energy for the entry of your highly evolved soul child who is coming soon. This child needed you to be ready for her and have your heart wide open to love her the way she needs to be loved in this lifetime. Your losses have prepared you well for this. In your meditation tonight, have a conversation with the spirits of your babies. Thank the babies who couldn't stay for helping you open your heart and appreciate the beauty of motherhood. Thank the baby who is coming to stay for giving you time to get ready to love her in the way you may not have been able to love her years ago. This is all divine order in action—even though it seems like tragedy now. Focus on shifting your energy to gratitude and love, and soon you will be holding a beautiful new baby in your arms.

Q: *Why do I feel so guilty about my wife's death? She died of cancer, so it wasn't my fault. But I keep feeling like "if only" I had made her go to the doctor sooner. . . .*

A: When someone dies, it is so incomprehensible to us that the person is gone that we search for a cause we can understand with our logical mind. As a result, whenever anyone dies, there's at least one person left behind who believes the death was his or her fault—true or not. Once you shift into your right-brain consciousness through meditation and embrace your spirituality, you'll see a bigger view. You'll understand that you and your wife were simply fulfilling a soul agreement you both made long before this lifetime began. Your guilt is very frustrating to her as she tries to reach out and comfort you. It's not how she wants you to feel. Embrace a bigger view, a deeper understanding, meditate daily, and when you think of her, feel love instead of guilt. She'll be delighted!

Q: *I never cry, and my therapist has told me that I need to cry to heal my grief. Why do I need to cry to heal?*

A: Crying releases endorphins (called the "feel-good hormone"); it creates chemical changes in the body that facilitate a sense of well-being. Crying also opens us up energetically. It shakes loose the painful feelings we're holding on to. A good cry opens the heart, and the heart must be opened to heal. How do you allow yourself to cry? Changing your daily routine and stepping out of your comfort zone is a good place to start. A new environment opens you up to experience your buried feelings. Go on a spiritual retreat weekend or take a vacation somewhere you've never been before. I strongly recommend starting and ending each day with the Break Your Heart Wide Open Meditation described on {page 87}. When you begin each day by feeling and releasing your grief, your days become happier and lighter, and you're able to move forward in a positive direction.

Q: *How do I get through my first Christmas without my loved one?*

A: Do something outside your normal routine for your first Christmas after your loved one has died, whether that means taking a wilderness trek, going on a spiritual retreat, or volunteering at your local homeless shelter. Don't try to have a normal Christmas, because you won't feel normal. Stay away from the usual parties and family get-togethers. They'll increase your pain and flood you with painful memories. You're not the same person you were last Christmas, and you need to shift your focus now. You're being called to embrace your spirituality and reinvent your life. Spend time in a spiritual community where the conversations are deep and meaningful. If you have children who want a normal Christmas, explain that you're all going to volunteer and help others this Christmas in honor of your loved one. Ask your children what their departed loved one would have wanted them to do in his or her name. For example, if your husband or wife loved animals, volunteer at the pet shelter. If your departed was a doctor, bring gifts to the patients and staff where he or she worked. This teaches a powerful lesson about healing; that we heal ourselves when we help others. Connecting to the higher self pulls us out of ego-driven victim-thinking— which is where grief dwells.

Q: *The anniversary of my daughter's death is coming up, and it makes me feel sick to my stomach. How will I get through that day and honor her?*

A: Recognize that this *is* a special day to honor her and don't try to ignore the day or follow your normal routine. You'll feel your departed loved one's presence all throughout this day. She'll be communicating with you and giving you signs of her presence. You want to be in a peaceful space to receive these messages and show her you're doing well. Begin your day with the Daily Reconnection Ritual described on {page 80}. This will help you connect with your departed daughter first thing in the morning. After meditating, go for a thirty-minute walk or run to get your chi (life-force energy) flowing. Your affirmation for this anniversary day is: "I'm living this day with my heart opened— knowing that my daughter is at my side and communicating with me. I will show her how well I'm doing and make her proud of me." If you go to work, take flowers or something beautiful such as a candle as a gift to your coworkers. Tell them you're honoring the day by giving beautiful things to people who've helped you get through the year. Use the powerful energy of your daughter's presence to bring joy to others. These acts will make you both happy as she watches from the other realms.

Q: *What about unfinished business—like forgiveness? My wife died suddenly, and I didn't get to say good-bye. This haunts me— especially because we were arguing the day she died. How do I move past this?*

A: She feels you worrying about this every day. It's frustrating for her that you're carrying this guilt. From her point of view, your guilt is ridiculous. She sees the depth and breadth of your relationship through many lifetimes, and has almost no memory of the insignificant final hours of this incarnation. Tonight, sit in meditation and light a candle for your wife. Tell her that since you didn't have a proper good-bye, you'll now say to her the things you wanted to say before she left. Say it all—express the love, pain, gratitude, and forgiveness. Offer it all up to her. Blow out the candle when you've finished. Know that she's heard all of it. Ask her for a dream or other message to validate that she heard you. If you don't receive a dream you can remember, ask for another sign that you will notice. Then pay attention and trust your intuition.

Q: *My boyfriend recently broke up with me, and the level of grief I'm feeling is way out of proportion. I think it's bringing up all my past grief, especially the grief of losing my father a few years ago.*

A: You bring up such a good point about grief triggering more grief. If we haven't embraced our true spiritual nature and recognized our losses as soul mate agreements, each new loss pushes us harder to remember our divine nature. The pain increases exponentially until we get the lesson. Use this time of grieving for your boyfriend to meditate and gain a more enlightened perspective on your journey. Become a student of all spiritual paths until you find what's true for you. Use my Break Your Heart Wide Open Meditation on {page 87} to release your pain each morning. Have a conversation with your departed father and ask for his guidance. Once you accept that your departed father still watches over you (which he does), you won't feel abandoned. You'll be able to view this breakup as another perfectly designed moment of divine order guiding you toward accomplishing your soul's mission for this lifetime.

Q: *My husband is dying. How can I best help him?*

A: By speaking the truth. (I've outlined a step-by-step process for helping loved ones cross over in chapter 12 of this book.) Discuss death openly with him. Ask him how he feels about dying and what he believes will happen when he crosses over. He needs to have that conversation with someone. Our souls know when we're about to leave, even if we're denying it outwardly. We long to tie up the loose ends with our loved ones. He'll want to review his memories with you. Follow the process I've outlined, and you'll help him experience a peaceful and fearless transition to the higher realms. This is the greatest final gift we can share with those we love.

Q: *How do I prepare myself for when he's gone?*

A: In your daily meditations, ask to be guided and protected through your grief. Ask for clarity about your soul's purpose—to have your meaningful work revealed clearly. Share honest conversations with your loved one today so you won't have regrets when he's passed on. Ask him how he wants you to carry on after he's gone. His soul knows that you must stay here. He'll try to give you guidance with whatever words he can find to get the message across. My husband was unable to speak at the end and struggled to scribble one word on a piece of paper: "gifted." As he handed it to me, he pointed at me with a power that gave me chills. I knew he was telling me I had to stay because I hadn't yet used my gifts to do my great work.

Part Three

Seeing Why You're Still Here and What to Do Now

Chapter Seven

THE SOUL MISSION
REVEALS YOUR GIFTS

Finding Your Golden Key to a New Life

When you chose this lifetime, you brought with you a Golden Key to open the door to your soul's mission—no matter how great the challenges you faced. Your key might be making music, talking to others, writing, dancing, running, creating beauty, cooking, or any talent that you've felt inside you from the beginning of this lifetime.

This Golden Key is the thing you go to when all else is lost. It's the thing you remember finding solace in as a child. And it's what you need to bring into your life now to find your next step.

Writing has always been my Golden Key; it opened every door for me. I wanted to be a writer from the time I was seven when my grandfather gave me an old black metal Royal typewriter. He put it on the table in front of me and explained how it worked. It had shiny black round keys rimmed in silver and smelled of ink and ribbon. It was the most beautiful thing I'd ever seen. I sat down and typed a story about a parade with a magical red balloon. My grandfather was delighted: "Hot damn! That girl's going to be a writer!"

I wrote poetry, short stories, science fiction, and murder mysteries all through childhood. By adolescence, I was writing full novels and had become the school poet, writing a poem for each issue of the school paper. One of my poems won a local award and was published in other school publications.

Writing saved my life. It was the only thing I was really good at, and it got me accepted into the University of Missouri to study journalism, which opened the door to pursue bigger dreams and, most important, to leave the South.

In college, I quickly learned that my introverted, sensitive, intuitive self was the furthest thing from a hard-nosed reporter capable of hunting down a story. I couldn't quite fit the journalist mold, so I dropped out of college to find my own way. Years later, I reenrolled in the University of Missouri to study psychology because I was fascinated by the mysteries of the human psyche. Teachers loved my papers and writing assignments, but I always struggled with the left-brain multiple- choice exams.

I put myself through college by becoming a Montessori preschool teacher. That allowed me to write "stories" about my students' academic and personal development, which I shared during conference time. I intuitively saw my students' great potentials and shared that vision with their parents, who loved it. Montessori teaching healed my underdeveloped left brain and helped me develop logic and linear thinking, which I sorely needed. As I taught young minds to grasp language, numbers, and practical thinking, I healed myself as well. Maria Montessori had studied theosophy (a blend of theology and philosophy) and so did I. Theosophy became my guiding light for embracing a bigger spiritual view of the world than my Catholic upbringing had provided.

In my early twenties, when my first young love broke my heart, I signed up for an Outward Bound Survival course off the coast of Maine. It was hardest thing I'd ever done, and it rebuilt my confidence. Impossibly, with nothing but sheer determination on my side, I became a Colorado Outward Bound mountaineering instructor and taught rock climbing and survival in the Rocky Mountains of Colorado—where I met my husband, Paul. Writing was still only a sideline, not something I was able to make a living from. I relentlessly tried to get published, to no avail.

By the time I was thirty and Paul had died, I'd written dozens of articles, screenplays, novels, and children's books, which had all been rejected by countless publishers. I felt like a failure as a writer—yet writing was still the one true gift I believed I had and the thing I felt most compelled to do. But I needed an income desperately, being widowed at thirty with bills to pay.

During my time with Paul, I had experienced many powerfully spiritual and intuitive awakenings. But how did those experiences apply to my life now? How was I to make a living from spirituality and intuition? In 1980, I saw no possibility of supporting myself from these right-brain gifts of writing or intuition.

Still determined to succeed as a writer, I took evening fiction writing and poetry classes at University of Colorado while trying to support myself as a fitness instructor. Teaching fitness was not a lucrative career in the early '80s, so I took on a paper route to bring in extra money. As you can imagine, this was not the happiest of times.

About a year after Paul died, I had a dream in which a beloved girlfriend walked up to me and handed me a journalism degree from University of Colorado. She said, "Here, it's time for you to do this."

I woke up knowing I needed to enroll in the journalism graduate school at CU and finally turn my love of writing into a career that would support me. I was not the same person I had been at nineteen, when I first tried journalism. So I signed up for classes the next day and slowly learned to be a reporter—covering city council meetings, crime stories, and court cases—because I had to.

I was so determined to make my living as a writer that I landed a reporting job at a local newspaper while still in journalism graduate school. The editor was a kind and wonderful man who truly saw who I was and understood my gifts. Even though he still needed the mundane news stories covered, he also asked me to write a personal story about the Boulder Hospice and include my story of Paul's death. I declined to write it for months. It seemed far too painful a story to tell. Finally, toward the end of my second semester of journalism school, he gave me a deadline.

Writing that painful story was the first time I found my voice as a journalist. It won a national writing award. (I've included that story in chapter 10 of this book). It created a buzz in the community and gave me a glimpse of how my writing could support me by telling heartfelt stories about the human struggle.

Eventually my passion for writing led me to a happy career as a magazine writer interviewing cancer survivors (such as Jill Ireland) and telling their stories. That led to a long, successful stint as editor of a magazine dedicated to healthy living. I took that journalism career as far as it would go—finally becoming the Vice President of Content for major health Web sites during the dot-com era of the late 1990s.

The crash of the dot-com world in 1999 stripped me bare of my journalism career and spurred a major life reinvention. I was a forty-eight-year-old single mom and couldn't get a job. Losing that career pushed me to find a new way of combining spiritual truth and intuition with writing, which led me to what I do today.

I tell you this to inspire you to embrace your Golden Key and never let it go. It will eventually open all the doors and get you where you're meant to be. Trust in divine order even when it feels like chaos. And say yes to each step only when it feels right in your heart.

The most helpful way to understand how to use your Golden Key is to study your soul's mission as described by Pythagoras, a mystic and the father of our modern number system. I've used his work as my gateway to understanding myself and everyone else since 1980.

I always knew I was here to write. But when I fully embraced Pythagoras's work and understood that my writing had to be in alignment with my soul's mission—to inspire others with new ideas and help raise consciousness—I began writing the right stuff. Only then did I become truly successful.

So let's consider what Pythagoras has to teach us.

Your Path . . .
You would not be experiencing a great loss today if you hadn't signed up for this life reinvention designed to occur exactly when it did. Your grief-driven reinvention will push you into your greatest work in a way that you may never have imagined. Or perhaps you once dreamt of doing something great, but dismissed it as an impossible dream. This is your moment to remember what you came here to do. The work of Pythagoras will clearly illuminate your next step toward fulfilling your potential.

Pythagoras first discovered a hidden code in 580 b.c., when he created the number system that we learned in math class— although our teachers never told us the whole story.

Pythagoras, who was the founder of a school for spiritual enlightenment, believed that numbers carry an energy or feeling, and that they're not just describing quantity. He taught his followers that when you add all the single digits in your date of birth, you find your destiny number, which reveals what you've come to accomplish. This destiny number provides a picture of the greatness you came to achieve, along with the potential pitfalls of your path. It reveals the nature of your true work and your many soul mate agreements.

Once you understand your soul's intention for this lifetime, it explains everything. You realize why you've always carried a big dream in your heart, loved certain people, and hungered for certain opportunities. You also recognize how fear and self-doubt have pulled you off your path and made you question your mission.

Remembering your destined path puts you in the positive, juicy flow of your life. It takes you to love and success. It's the map you've been looking for. And it's all hidden in your birth date.

You may be wondering how your date of birth could be so destined? Perhaps your doctor scheduled your mom's Cesarean delivery in his calendar based on his busy practice. Or perhaps you were born three months early. How, you ask, can this be destiny?

Here's the answer: You came here on purpose on *your* schedule!

Your soul chose the exact moment of entry just as it will choose the exact moment of exit (even though you're not consciously aware of this). When the doctor looked at his crowded datebook and scribbled in the date of your Cesarean birth, you were holding the pencil.

Let's explore the powerful truths your date of birth reveals. . . .

Pythagoras's Number System
We reduce all numbers to the digits *1* through *9,* except for three cosmic vibrations symbolized by the master numbers *11, 22,* and *33.*

All other numbers are reduced to the basic digits 1 through 9 by adding the digits of the entire number together.

For example, the number 43 equals 7 (4 + 3 = 7).

The number 10 equals 1 (1 + 0 = 1).

Example of a Birth Path Calculation
For the birth date of October 16, 1980:

Month = October equals 10, equals 1 (1 + 0)
Date = 16 equals 7 (1 + 6)
Year = 1980 equals 9 (1 + 9 + 8 + 0 = 18), (1 + 8 = 9)
Total of month plus date plus year equals 17 (1 + 7 + 9), which equals 8 (1 + 7)
Birth path number = 8

The Master Soul Numbers
The master numbers of 11, 22, and 33 represent sacred birth paths designed to help humanity evolve. Those numbers are not reduced to a single digit in the final birth path calculations. (But they are reduced to

single digits when calculating your final sum. For example, the month of November digits down to a 2 to determine your final birth path number.)

Example of a Master Soul Birth Path Calculation

For the birth date of September 15, 1951:

Month = September equals 9 Date = 15 equals 6 (1 + 5)
Year = 1951 equals 7 (1 + 9 + 5 + 1 = 16), (1 + 6 = 7)
Total of month plus date plus year equals 22 (9 + 6 + 7) Master soul birth path number = 22

This is also referred to as a 22/4 path, since the 22 is always connected to the 4 path. (Similarly, the 11 path is referred to as 11/2 path, and the 33 path is referred to as a 33/6 path.)

Three Ways of Adding Birth Dates

It's important to add each birth date three different ways to check your addition and to look for hidden master soul path numbers.

This is especially important if you've arrived at a 2, 4, or 6 birth path calculation. These birth paths often contain a hidden 11, 22, or 33 path if added two other ways. If the master soul number is "hidden" in this way, it means this person will choose when they're ready to step up to their great work—usually later in life.

If the final sum of the birth date is 11, 22, or 33 just one of the three ways you add it, that means the person is on the master soul journey of 11, 22, or 33.

For example, the birth date May 1, 1960, results in the 22 master soul life birth path. Two out of three ways reveal a 22/4 path, while the third way reveals a 13/4.

These are the three ways you would add this birth date to discover that two out of three ways reveal a 22/4 path while the third way reveals a 13/4.

Traditional First Method
May = 5
1 = 1
1960 = 16 = 7
Total of 13 = birth path number 4 (1 + 3)

Second Method
5 + 1 + 1960 = 1966
Total of 1966 = master soul birth path 22/4 (1 + 9 + 6 + 6)

Third Method
5 + 1 + 1 + 9 + 6 + 0 = master soul birth path number 22/4

Another example follows for September 15, 1951.

Traditional First Method
September = 9
15 = 6
1951 = 7
Total = master soul birth path number 22 (9 + 6 + 7)

Second Method
1951 + 15 + 9 = 1975

Total = master soul birth path number 22 (1 + 9 + 7 + 5)

Third Method
9 + 1 + 5 + 1 + 9 + 5 + 1 = 31 = birth path number 4 (3 + 1)

Another Example of the Third Method
Using President Barack Obama's birth date of August 4, 1961: 8
+ 4 + 1 + 9 + 6 + 1 = 29 = 2 + 9 = 11

His birth path is a hidden 11/2 master soul path, meaning that 11/2 is the final calculation only when added with the third method. The other two methods both result in a final calculation of 20/2. Because it's a "hidden" master soul number, it means he chose when he was ready to step up to do his great work. Until then, he could fit easily into conventional careers without revealing his true spiritual essence.

Calculate your birth path from your date of birth, using all three of the methods displayed above.

First method result:

Second method result:

Third method result:

All three methods should arrive at the same final number—even if you discover you're on a master soul birth path of 11, 22, or 33. Those master soul birth path calculations result in the consistent final combinations of 11/2, 22/4, or 33/6—at least one of the ways you add the birth date. The other two ways may result in various other two-digit numbers that when added together total 2, 4, or 6. (Examples are 20/2, 13/4 or 15/6.)

Your birth month:
Your birth date:
Your birth year:
Total:
Reduced to a single digit:
Your birth path number:

Note that zero is more than a placeholder in numerology. It's called a potentiator—meaning the zero makes the number in front of it (or behind it) stronger. If your birth path calculation arrives at the number 2020, each zero strengthens the two in front of it— making this number digit down to a 22/4 master soul birth path. The same is true for 1010 or 3030, which become 11/2 and 33/6.

Positive and Negative Meanings of Numbers

In Pythagoras's system, every number from 1 through 9 has a positive and negative vibration (which shows its great potential and challenges):

1—Leadership, vision, independence *or* loneliness, self-doubt, arrogance

2—Intuition, understanding, detail *or* dependency, paranoia, obsession with meaningless details

3—Self-expressive, creative, uplifting *or* coldhearted, overintellectual, irresponsible

4—Self-discipline, strength, determination, practicality *or* too practical, lost in drudgery and routine

5—Change, sensuality, freedom, passion *or* overindulgence, addictions, impulsive, uncentered

6—Social consciousness, healer, teacher *or* slave to others' needs, supercritical of loved ones

7—Intellectual, spiritual focus, wise, dignified, refined *or*
isolated, hypersensitive, skeptical

8—Power, wealth, accomplishment, generosity *or* abusive, manipulative, controlling, hiding from power

9—Humanitarian, accomplished, artistic *or* bitter, blameful, focused on past

Master Soul Numbers

11—Intuitive, artistic, humanitarian, healer *or* too sensitive, egocentric

22—Inspired visionary, practical genius *or* greedy, abusive, lost in drudgery

33—Visionary artist, clairvoyant, master healer *or* hypersensitive, lost in addictions, disconnected from others

Why Does Your Path Matter?

Once you find your path, you understand your soul mission and what you came to do. It reveals your Golden Key for this lifetime. Your path illuminates your reason for still being here in the physical world even though your loved one has moved on. By embracing the soul mission, you rise to the challenge of your lifetime and fulfill your purpose. Only then are you able to join your loved one in the highest realms

Birth Path 1

You've done nothing wrong to cause this heartbreak you're experiencing. You just need a little space and freedom to realize and follow your independent heart. You're a visionary, a born leader—this is your Golden Key. Self-doubt is your downfall, and your grief has probably triggered it. Once you get on your feet, your visionary ideas will help thousands of people.

Stop listening to what everyone tells you to do to recover from this loss. Take your own path and do it your way. Start meditating to hear your inner guidance. And get back on your feet. You designed your body and its great strength to carry you forward no matter what, and now is not the time to lie down. Stand up!

Speak your truth, follow your intuition, and go your independent way—even if that means walking away from old friends and security. You'll find true financial security and happiness only when you're doing your great work, even if it's unconventional.

This is not an easy path, but you knew that coming in. So you brought a vast array of gifts to use as your tools for getting it done. These include boundless strength, courage, natural leadership, charisma, honesty, stage presence, brilliance, and independence.

Your challenge, of course, is the opposite of your mission. That enormous pool of self-doubt you dip into daily is also your fuel. Its purpose is to motivate you. You've spent too many nights in the depths of pain—wondering if you're worthy of taking another breath. Let me assure you, we all wait for your vision. We need you to take your place at the head of the line. Don't disappoint us. No one else can do your job and lead us to a better way of living.

This mission requires you to speak up even when that seems the most terrifying thing you can do. The more you share your wisdom, the more powerful your voice becomes—until it becomes the song of compassion and wisdom that changes our world.

At some point, you may decide it's all too hard and lonely and you need to hide out. It's your choice. Every choice can and will be made until you get it right. You'll sometimes struggle to understand where other people fit in your journey. You'll feel wounded when others don't understand your power. You may choose to strike back and hurt them, or distance yourself from their love. This will take time and energy and it will lead you off track.

Eventually, you'll take your place at the center of the room as the enlightened teacher, trailblazer, and shaman who guides us to secret knowledge. You're the one we trust to teach us a better way, and to help us move past our own self-doubt to fulfill our missions. Your story of pain, loss, and recovery is meant to be shared. Your wisdom will encourage others. Speak your truth and you will succeed.

To Recover, You Need
Reconnection with your own higher self. This means getting away from everyone and everything you know—even if it's just for a weekend retreat. As you get out of your routine, you will connect to your higher self through nature, spirituality, meditation, and writing, and you will hear your own inner truth again. That's the only voice you should listen to.

Don't underestimate the lesson of your loss: to nudge you to embrace your highest self and your spiritual soul mission. Your career needs to be meaningful, which in your case means leading others to new discoveries. Inspired leadership is your Golden Key. If you're working at a corporate job with little power to do things independently, it's time for a major career reinvention! Your work is meant to lead the way for others—as a consultant, teacher, coach, writer, or entrepreneur. If you're pursuing an artistic career, now is the time to teach others what you've already learned in this lifetime.

Birth Path 2
The loss of a loved one is especially hard for you because you merge so deeply with those you love. This great sensitivity means that you still feel your loved one even though they've crossed into another

world. This, my dear, is your Golden Key to recovery. Daily intuitive connection with your departed will heal you and help you realize that connecting to others as a therapist, healer, or intuitive is your mission and should be the way you make your money. As you embrace spiritual knowledge and open your powerful heart, grief will slip away and you'll embrace the beauty of your sensitivity. You'll finally realize it's your greatest gift.

Because you manifest all your challenges and gifts through your interactions with others in the workplace and at home, healing yourself requires daily connection with friends, family, and your departed. Isolation is not healthy for you. Volunteer in a shelter for abused women or at a day care center. Your gifts will create a golden light around you and inspire clients to seek you out.

You'll soon have a posse of friends and coworkers who rely on you for counsel. I hope your powerful sensitivity and intuition will inspire you to become a therapist, teacher, or healer. Your most powerful work will be to embrace others in your loving energy. Ultimately, you'll become a beacon of compassion and support to those you're responsible for and widely recognized for your compassionate sensitivity.

To Recover, You Need
Connection with people! Being home alone or isolated in a cubicle at work will only increase your pain. Get out of your house and away from your desk. Get up and offer a helping hand or a healing conversation to anyone you meet. Making a sacred connection with others is your Golden Key. I suggest going to luncheon networking events or charity benefits—anything that gives you an opportunity to share your healing voice with others.

Birth Path 11
You have a huge connection to the other realms that enables you to channel in love, intuition, and healing. This divine connection is your Golden Key. Grief is your wake-up call to become the divine healer and light-being you came here to be.

Instead of crying about your departed, show them you will become a channel of artistic and spiritual inspiration for others. Make them proud. They know you're an angelic being. They want to see you use this gift to help others. This is your chance to get it right and make your living from your amazing gifts!

You vibrate on such an amped-up frequency that it sets you apart. When you enter a room, your energy demands attention. Use this charisma to share positive, helpful, and inspiring ideas. Refuse to speak hurtful words to others, even when you feel wounded.

You can intuit every feeling present in a room and you sense what everyone is thinking. This is your gift, though you may not see it as a gift at first. In your lowest moments you might feel paranoid—as if you're going through life with no skin— vulnerable, exposed, and overwhelmed by feelings. Remember, this is your gift and not your flaw.

Without spiritual focus, you'll waste your life feeling paranoid, wounded, or trying to please everyone rather than following your own unique mission. Fitting in and being like everyone else is not an option for you. This grief and heartbreak you're experiencing is meant to get you to own your gifts and give up the conventional mask you've been wearing.

Find a daily spiritual practice that works for you and do it consistently. I recommend meditation because it quiets your mind and allows you to deepen your pathway to the divine realms. You'll need to establish that connection every day and use it as a time to ask your departed to wrap you in love so that you can carry on with your great work. Meditation and intuitive connection with your loved one will provide the strength needed to overcome your sensitivity, open your heart, and accomplish your great mission.

Your mission is truly unique. You're capable of the highest forms of artistic creation. As a speaker or writer, you'll tap into inspiring ideas the world needs to transform itself. You belong on the stage sharing your spiritual message, your story of healing, and inspiring us to live in more enlightened ways. To say you shine is an understatement. Your presence leaves others breathless.

If you correctly use these gifts for their highest good, you can change the consciousness of humanity in your lifetime. You'll attract great praise and criticism as you live up to your brilliant path. Be wary of getting lost in tangents, or being overly sensitive, or you won't accomplish everything you came to do. Embrace your abundant intuition and trust it to navigate you successfully on this path—overriding your fear and doubt at every turn.

To Recover, You Need

Daily connection with your spirituality, higher self, and departed loved ones! Start every morning with a twenty-minute meditation, and your pain will diminish. You'll feel your loved one's arms around you and you'll know that they're with you. This will motivate you to step away from meaningless actions and empty careers. You'll know in your heart how gifted you are, and you'll someday embrace intuition as your Golden Key and use it to teach others to see their loved ones in the other realms.

Birth Path 3

Get out of your head and stop analyzing every feeling—from devastating grief to passionate love. Feel it all—from joy to pain! Move your body to get your feelings flowing. Open your heart and connect to your highest self through dance, creativity, writing, and play.

This grief is meant to break you wide open and fill your heart with compassion. A life lived in the mind is not what your soul intended. You're capable of enormous love and of using that love to inspire others!

Your Golden Key involves creativity, artistic expression, and leading others (as a teacher, writer, or entrepreneur) to find their own unique self-expression. This requires inner work as you quiet your brilliant mind, open your heart, and learn to feel.

Words are essential to the work you came to do. Tell your story of grief and recovery! Through exploration of the written word, you'll find your ultimate gift as a speaker and enlightened writer. Your books, inventions, and other works of creativity will someday be held in reverence as examples of great genius and inspiration.

Your challenge will be feeling what you feel. Your cerebral viewpoint disconnects you from the world and from your higher self. Physical movement is essential because it quiets your overactive mind and reestablishes connection to your higher self. Try yoga, tai chi, qigong, and other types of healing movement to open your heart.

Your gift for movement, music, and visual design makes you an awesome athlete, dancer, designer, musician, or choreographer— as long as you remember to bring your feelings into the work.

The world needs your voice. You intended to share these powerful gifts through your work—not keep them to yourself. Speaking and teaching are perfect opportunities for moving toward your true work.

You can move energy in a room, on the stage, through your body, or through music and writing. The purpose of these gifts is to heal others in pain. As you mature into this lifetime and embrace the lesson of your grief, you'll learn to cherish your feelings as much as ideas, and all your creative endeavors will have a divine intent.

You need a deep spiritual connection to balance out your mind, along with daily physical movement to strengthen your intuition. Your grief may cause mental exhaustion, which will lead you to a spiritual awakening. You'll realize that you can't find all answers through the mind, and that truth lies deep inside your higher consciousness—beyond the limitations of thought. Indeed, the answer you're looking for lives in your mostly hidden yet compassionate heart.

To Recover, You Need
To feel your pain and release it! Now is *not* the time to bury your head in analytical thinking and distance yourself from emotion. Your witty

cynicism is *not* what's needed now, nor will it help you or those around you deal with the pain of grief. Do the Break Your Heart Wide Open Meditation each morning to open your heart, feel the pain, and release it. Without this daily practice, you'll shut down your emotions to avoid feeling the pain of your loss. Open your heart and use it to inspire your brilliantly creative efforts. Use your Golden Key of creative self-expression to produce your most divinely inspired work! Moving your body with dance, yoga, or athletic activities will help you move out of your head. Open your heart and feel; the lesson of your grief will be illuminated, and your life will unfold on its path.

Birth Path 4

Your great integrity and sense of humor will help you move forward through this painful time. Use your Golden Key of strength and determination to dive wholeheartedly into your career and accomplish your great work. Your grief is truly the fuel you need to accomplish your mission. The time to take action is now! Remember to include laughter, fun, and relaxation in your hardworking life or you could exhaust yourself and damage your health.

You possess more natural courage, honesty, and determination than others. Your best choice is to embrace the challenge of hard work as your opportunity 0for spiritual and emotional growth through this devastating loss. Try not to get overwhelmed.

Your positive attitude will lead to great happiness and success. The courage and strength you build in this lifetime will serve you and the world as you use it to accomplish feats impossible for others.

Your strength, focus, and willpower can accomplish any challenge, from climbing Mount Everest to running a newsroom, or building homes from scratch. You always get it done, no matter how big the job or short the deadline. You're meant to pursue and succeed at impossible dreams when others can't. Never limit your expectations, and always say yes to challenges.

In your time of greatest pain, you'll be drawn to others with strength and fortitude, and you'll have little patience for trivia and superficiality.

You'll feel happiest when pushing yourself to physical and mental extremes. This exertion makes you feel powerful and alive again.

I suggest massive doses of physical exercise and movement to heal your loss. The worst course of action for you is to do nothing. Inactivity creates huge discordance and self-doubt because it's not what you came to experience this time around. It makes you feel weak—which is not in alignment with your mission.

Whenever you feel victimized by your loss, embrace your spiritual nature. This will help you see the bigger picture and choose tasks worthy of your great fortitude and dedication. You'll pursue spiritual truth with the same powerful determination and fortitude that others use to climb mountains. This inner strength will guide you accurately to a spiritual path that will heal your pain.

You see and speak the truth without hesitation. This honesty will both serve you and get you in trouble. You may become disappointed in others who don't speak the truth and have less integrity than you. They'll catch you off guard because you assume the same good intentions in others as you carry in this lifetime.

Your trusting nature and enormous sense of responsibility are unique, and you'll realize eventually how rare those gifts are. Be careful whom you trust—especially when sharing your pain. Follow your intuition when choosing work projects and loved ones. This will ensure that you'll be using your terrific determination to accomplish your greatest work.

To Recover, You Need
To dig deep and accomplish your great work, run your marathon, and never look back! Write the book, study at the university, make your film, climb your mountain. Using strength to accomplish whatever you put your mind to is your Golden Key to the life you desire. Just don't sit around doubting yourself. Wasting time won't make you happy.

Don't be seduced into pain-numbing relationships or addictions. They will increase your pain in the long run. You're here to accomplish what others only dream of doing, and this grief is your nudge to get it done. Find a brilliant, intuitive friend to discuss the meaning of life with, begin your greatest work, and embrace your spiritual path 200 percent!

Birth Path 22
It's time to embrace your spirituality and use it as your Golden Key to uplift and inspire others. This is why you signed up for this devastating loss. By spirituality, I don't mean just reading a book or two. I mean daily connection to the divine through meditation and intense spiritual practice. It's time to embrace your intuition profoundly enough to build your great work around it.

You've been driven to do something great with your life from the time you were very young. And you're acutely aware of your unique perspective and how it differs from mainstream thought. Let this pain fuel you to move forward and succeed at something that inspires and changes our world.

It's time to quit trying to fit in and be someone you're not. You've hidden your unusual gifts in order to be loved. But the world will embrace you for who you truly are when you share your story through your great work.

There is nothing average or normal about you. Your frequency is several notches higher, more attuned and intuitive than anyone else is around you. Because of this contrast, you may have doubted yourself in the past. There is nothing wrong with you!

First, you must find your spiritual practice and use it every day as your fountain of inspiration and power. This will help you navigate a world that seems crazy, from your perspective. Sharing your unique viewpoint is your true work!

When you open your heart and share the enormous love you carry for humanity, it wraps the world in peace and forgiveness. When you shut down, your cold power wounds everyone.

You won't ever want to settle for a mundane career—and that's on purpose. You don't belong there. When you take that path, it never works out. Your high-frequency presence sabotages all attempts at having a conventional life. That's a good thing!

Your vision of a better world is your gift. Don't dismiss it or waste time criticizing the way things are now. Tap into your enormous pool of inspiration and find a way to use your vision as the foundation for your work. That mission is the one you came to share.

This grief is your moment of reinvention. You need partners and friends whose conversations leave you feeling uplifted and inspired to do something bigger.

You'll have the strength of the 4 combined with the inspiration and brilliance of the 22. Use that amazing combination to accomplish your mission, making significant, inspired contributions to the way we think and live.

Your powerful 4-path strength is necessary for this journey of recovery, so be sure to nurture your physical health through exercise and healthy food. Alternatives will always attract you— especially alternative medicine, which you'll find very helpful in this lifetime.

Your salvation lies in seeing the big picture, following your inspiration, opening your heart, and not getting lost in details, drudgery, or routine.

Your highest work requires stepping out of the confines of convention— into alternative worlds of knowledge, spirituality, intuition, and healing. You're creating a body of work that will be honored and followed long after you exit this life.

To Recover, You Need
To do your work, the work you signed up for that will enlighten the world! Your Golden Key is to inspire us all with your paradigm-shifting ideas. Nothing will ease your pain as much as inspiration and accomplishment. Embracing daily spiritual practice is a necessary step

to healing. Remember, your departed loved one is watching and knows you have lots of work to do. They're ready to help! Don't frustrate them by giving in to indulgences that lead nowhere. You don't need a resting place now. That will only increase your pain. Just do it!

Birth Path 5

You need to dig deep in your core and embrace a new spiritual perspective, or this pain will lead you into destructive behaviors. You'll get lost in addictions, indulgences, and passions— following your propensity to learn all your lessons through the flesh. You have enormous personal charisma, and this is your Golden Key. But charisma can also lead you down the dark side if you're not using your presence to help others. Your indulgences can put you in rehab or, worse, endanger your life. But you're here for a reason and you need to understand that. It's not your time to exit the physical world.

Your wide-open sensuality and powerful passion are designed to open your heart. Your mission is to drink fearlessly from the cup of life—learning everything there is to learn about the physical realm and experiencing it through every cell. Earthly pleasures, from food to music and drugs, will seduce you, and you may get lost in self-indulgence.

Early childhood pain and abuse may have caused you to shut down your wise spirit and hungry heart. It's time to wake up. You came to this lifetime to embrace courage and step out of bounds. You're capable of sharing big love and healing through your work. But fear will shut your heart right down and pull you far off path.

Everyone is attracted to you. Abundant opportunities flow in your direction. This is all designed to teach you to make right choices for your soul's evolution and your highest good. Though you may choose the experiential school of hard knocks to learn these lessons, it's not necessary if you trust your boundless intuition. You sense everything and know things you shouldn't know. Trust that. It's your inner guidance system trying to make the journey easier. Your mind is unreliable, but your gut is always right.

You're definitely not suited for routine or convention. When you find yourself buried in it, you're off path. Freedom, expansion, adventure, and fearlessness feed your soul. Change is your most powerful ally. Embrace the energy of adventure and courage, because that's what you came to master. Say yes to new experiences even when they scare you. Your acceptance of these challenges will put you on your true path.

You'll find salvation in a rich spiritual perspective that grounds you in health and sanity. Only then will you be able to fulfill your intention of serving others who lose themselves in fear and illusions. However, embracing spirituality will be tough for you at first, since you tend to believe only in what you can see with your eyes and touch with your hands You may have to hit bottom from physical indulgences before you look beyond the physical world for meaning and purpose. Your great work will provide love and nurturing for those who've fallen off the edges. Your powerful compassion can heal the world when you let it.

You belong in the alternatives—from alternative health careers to adventurous travel and outdoor lifestyles. Yet you need meaning and purpose to anchor you, or life will become chaotic and could make you sick. Ultimately, you're here to help those who struggle with fear and lack of spiritual focus. You'll provide healing and comfort for those who flounder on the fringes of life and help them find purpose and meaning as you've found yours. You'll be the light of encouragement and truth for the world when you share your powerful and unconventional wisdom.

To Recover, You Need
Self-discipline and courage! It's time to make some big changes in your life and find your solid inner strength and wisdom. If you hide out now and bury your pain in addictions, you're just making life harder. Realize that you have a great mission to help others! Use your Golden Key of charisma to get everyone to listen to your ideas. Tell your story of pain and recovery! Heal those who wallow in indulgences. Become the voice of courage and change—even when those things terrify you. Courage is the only road to take and the only way to accomplish what you came here to do.

Birth Path 6

It's time for you to become the healer you came here to be. This grief is what you asked for to help you remember your mission. Put your focus on the world, the community, and the needs of others. Healing and helping others are your Golden Key and the antidote to your pain. Explore great artistic and philosophical ideas to rewire your brain. Use your healing and artistic gifts to help others instead of using your rock-star beauty to manipulate.

Your presence is angelic and gives you charisma that you can use to either heal the world with your enormous heart or slide down a dark path of self-destruction. It's your choice. And you may need to experience both sides before choosing to heal.

Your boundless gifts—especially the creative ones—allow you to pursue the artistic genius or gifted athlete path. You have profound intuition and the ability to sense energy. But without spirituality as your anchor, you may become untethered and unsuccessful.

If you're grieving today, it's because you forgot that your heart is for healing others' pain. Shine that love and compassion out to everyone you meet, and your life will blossom.

Ultimately, your soul's evolution occurs when you open your powerful heart and feel compassion, even for the imperfections of humanity. You'll heal and inspire your family, community, and world—moving from indulgent artist/athlete to enlightened healer/teacher/politician. You may not realize your greatest work until later in life.

True spirituality must be at the core of your life to keep you from crazy obsessions and focusing on others' imperfections. Your global consciousness will inspire you to work for justice and social causes, but you can get lost in the anger and blame of self- righteousness and risk becoming fanatical and destructive if your spiritual core isn't strong.

Home and family are essential to your happiness, and you may marry young. Beware of losing yourself in family needs and forgetting to grow as a person. If you're not healed, you can't help anyone else. You must remember who you are and get your own needs met to be fulfilled and happy.

To Recover, You Need
Forgiveness and gratitude! You've sometimes blamed others for your losses and ignored the lesson of your grief. Once you embrace your masterful healing gifts as your Golden Key to the life you desire, you become the compassionate leader at the front of the room—healing all of us with your grace and kindness. Your wise presence will make you very successful as a spiritual guide for others.

Birth Path 33
You're on a highly sensitive and gifted lifetime journey. This highly evolved and enlightened path is sometimes called the "Christ path." You have the highest frequency a soul can carry in this physical realm. Your Golden Key is your wide-open channel to the divine.

Grief may open you up to the highest realms in a way that could completely disconnect you from reality. You don't have much of a tether to this physical realm anyway, and unless you embrace your spirituality and use it to guide your everyday life, you may end up doing a stint either in the loony bin or the rehab center.

Remember the reason for your gift! You dance in the ethers to bring spiritual and intuitive guidance to the world. Your charisma and artistic gifts must be used to make a difference in the world or you'll lose your way through psychosis or addiction.

You chose this path to use love, wisdom, artistic talents, and clairvoyance to transform consciousness through your work. It's a big task but you're completely capable of success.

You're loaded with personality, beauty, and charisma on purpose. You have the most compassionate heart found on Planet Earth and you came here for big spiritual development for yourself and the world. As an artist, you have an unfettered pipeline to inspiration and an unmatched ability to download whatever guidance you desire for your creations.

When you finally become a healer or gifted artist, you'll be the clairvoyant, shaman, energy master, and intuitive who creates a new form of spiritual healing for the world. If you focus on this task, you can put an end to all disease of the body and soul.

Your challenge is as great as your gifts. With your unrestrained clairvoyance, intuition, and sensitivity, falling off the edges of the world is a definite possibility. This is why you must ground yourself in the highest spiritual awareness, stay far away from dark arts, and never touch a drop of alcohol or drugs. These vices can make your mission unobtainable and fill you with delusions that waste your time here on Earth.

To Recover, You Need
Prayer, meditation, and daily service to others. Connecting to the divine will mend your heart. This loss has occurred to remind you that you're not here to be like everyone else. You have huge work to do, and this is your moment. A spiritually evolved perspective is your Golden Key. To heal your pain, you must heal others. Read the lives of great saints including Mother Teresa and Saint Francis of Assisi. You're not required to sacrifice yourself, but you are here to save everyone else. Forgiveness would be a good place to start.

Birth Path 7
You're hungry for the truth, and this grief will spur you to either find enlightenment or become a deeply cynical and lost soul. It's your choice. Your Golden Key is your ability to see beyond the illusion and find answers about why you're here and who you really are. Embrace spirituality, intuition, and higher consciousness as your new perspective.

Moving forward requires basing your career on higher thought and spiritual insight. Release the cynicism and doubt. Because of your need for beauty and perfection, surround yourself with flowers and color to help you heal. Release the details and see the bigger picture of your life. This pain is designed to help you see that perfection does not exist in the physical world—only in the unseen worlds. Embrace your true intuitive gifts and use them in your work.

You chose this lifetime to bridge the physical and divine realms—to live in the physical world without losing your spiritual connection. Your greatest work is to meld these two worlds through art, music, and intuition. Your brilliant creativity comes from your unique ability to channel inspiration from the highest realms. This gift can change the world if you allow it to manifest completely through your work.

You've always been intent on learning why things are the way they are. Your insatiable intellect has pushed you to pursue the highest knowledge. Spirituality (not religion) will someday heal your sensitive soul and lift you out of negativity. Embracing love rather than sarcasm opens your creativity and fuels your great work.

If you find yourself lost in grief, it's because you're shut off from your own spiritual connection. You, more than anyone, need your spiritual pipeline opened up and flowing freely. Without it, you can become a bitter, fearful perfectionist finding flaws in anyone who gets close—terrified of this world and its unpredictable experiences.

Your goal is to learn that true perfection exists only in the highest realms and not here in the physical world. This lesson could take your entire lifetime to master because you're so driven to find perfection in the details. Yet this endless pursuit of meaningless perfection never makes you happy.

Your exceptionally refined energy makes you unsuited for most big business careers. Your pristine mind, which is capable of great learning, will urge you into finance, law, science, or religious studies where you're encouraged to ask "Why?" But even those fields will eventually feel limited and restrictive.

Your search for the truth will drive you to recognize that intuition and spiritual wisdom are your greatest gifts. Once you embrace that knowledge, anything you want to accomplish is possible.

Spending time outdoors in nature will probably be your first step toward embracing your higher self. You don't truly belong in this world, and much of the goings-on here will disgust you, but you came on purpose to help raise consciousness. Remember you're a visitor with a divine mission, and don't get pulled into the drama.

The spiritual and mystical will always call you, and therein lies your ultimate fulfillment. You'll be happiest when you have plenty of time alone to reconnect to your higher self.

Ultimately, you'll be the wise artist, writer, spiritual guide, and sacred teacher. You'll translate divine knowledge for the rest of us without having to live and work in the fray of human struggle.

To Recover, You Need
Quiet and reflection. Contemplation is the balm your soul needs to heal this loss and find answers to your painful questions. You'll recover quickly if you focus on spiritual practices, write your innermost thoughts, and study the teachings of the greatest spiritual guides. Read, write, and meditate. You'll feel at peace in nature. And when you've fully embraced this contemplative lifestyle, true healing will begin. Daily communication with your departed will come easily to you. Seeing the great spiritual truth of our shared human journey is your gift and your Golden Key. Telling that story to others is what you're here to do.

Birth Path 8
What a powerful life you came here to live, and this grief is your soul's nudge to fully step into that greatness. Owning your power is your Golden Key to a successful life. Playing victim or being abusive are both signs that you're avoiding the lesson at hand. This is your moment to embrace generosity, truth, and a relentless spiritual focus.

You're a truly brave and wise old soul, and you've already developed spiritual wisdom and genius in other lifetimes. When you chose this incarnation, you tackled the most difficult lesson that humans can take on: How do I own my power in every area of life and use it generously to empower others? Every lesson of your lifetime will be embodied in that simple question.

Your grieving heart is your greatest fuel to help you find your power and master the game of money (rather than avoiding it). You're more than capable of doing this even though it terrifies you.

On this journey, you've experienced every pitfall, from abuse and manipulation to sabotage and greed. Ultimately, you'll learn from these challenges and become abundantly successful, respected, and generous.

The only way to succeed at this mission is to step up to the plate. Thinking big is your only option. In this lifetime, you're not allowed to hide out for very long in any area of your life. You will be called to stand up for yourself in every relationship, starting from childhood. We see your greatness even when you don't.

Since you're here to experience great wealth and power, many opportunities to head in that direction will come your way. Just say yes even when you're afraid. Someday your success will enable you to do your greatest work—funding the causes you care about and helping millions of people who struggle in fear and poverty. Then you'll come full circle to fulfill your soul's intention for this lifetime. You'll have mastered one of the final and hardest lessons of human incarnations.

To Recover, You Need
To become truly powerful and independent—financially, emotionally, and spiritually! This is the point of your pain. Hiding out is not allowed, and if your spouse has crossed over leaving you penniless, that's on purpose! This is your moment to shine and accomplish what you came here to do. Be bold! Use the Golden Key of this powerful lifetime to step

fearlessly into your great work. You'll become the generous millionaire you're meant to be.

Birth Path 9

You already have one foot in the other realms. This grief is designed to help you master your final achievement in the physical world—surrendering everything to compassion, love, and forgiveness. Wisdom is your Golden Key to success. You've developed enormous spiritual and intuitive gifts over many past lifetimes. And you've already risen above many painful challenges.

This loss is the ultimate challenge for you; forgiveness is required now more than ever. Slipping into bitterness will be a temptation. Arrogance is your greatest flaw. But bitterness and arrogance only keep you from accomplishing your soul's true intention. Open your heart in ultimate surrender to what you don't yet know. A wide-open heart will move you quickly through the pain and allow your wisdom to shine through!

This ultimate lifetime ties up the loose ends of your karma and teaches you to live in tune with your highest self and pass your soul's final exam. You're asked to face heartbreak with compassion, loss with understanding, and disappointment with wisdom. It's time to realize you're always the wise old soul in the room, here to guide others. That carries responsibility. Take your place on the stage and teach this wisdom to others. You still have a huge humanitarian mission to accomplish, and it's time to move forward to the next step.

If your grief is weighing you down today, ask yourself if it's because you let loss and disappointment turn you into a bitter, blameful person, and you forgot to do your humanitarian work in the world. If you can truly say that you've released past grudges and disappointments, you're fulfilling your mission!

You're charismatic and brilliant enough that on the surface you look great. But deep inside is where the true work is needed—to release the arrogance and cynicism you still carry inside from painful past incarnations. To help you fulfill that mission, this lifetime presents many great teachers and opportunities for growth. You'll have many broken relationships to heal. Feeling your pain and releasing it to its highest good will open your heart to true love and success.

The charisma and skills you've gathered over so many lifetimes may confuse you, causing you to waste time in addictions and indulgences attracted by your personal beauty and presence. Your free spirit, enormous creativity, broad knowledge, wisdom, and compassion always make you the center of attention, but you must use this power for good rather than for manipulation.

Forgiveness and gratitude will serve you every day of this journey. Each time you master an inner challenge, your life will unfold in a joyful way as you prepare to exit the cycle of human incarnations. To graduate, you must surrender to your highest self and open your heart.

Inspire others with your compassion for the human condition and your deep understanding of spiritual truths. Your great work is humanitarian and service-oriented. Mysticism, music, and art intrigue you because of your ability to tap into the divine realms.

Practice sacred amnesia and forget anything or anyone who has ever wounded you. Reach for the future and finish this lifetime with grace and wisdom. You always intended to finish it strong.

To Recover, You Need

Daily spiritual connection and work that serves the world. If your work is meaningless, you're off path, and your pain will stop you from living the life you came to live. Wisdom is your Golden Key. Share your many wise lessons through your work, become a powerful teacher and writer, and speak for those who suffer in silence. Become the guide to our shared unrealized potential as spiritual beings on a journey of evolution.

Chapter Eight

YOUR GRIEF CYCLES OF REINVENTION

If you're facing a painful loss today, you'll understand your next step more clearly when you study your reinvention points. Looking back at this lifetime, you've probably recognized cycles of beginnings and endings, deaths and rebirths—all similar to the seasons of growth found in the natural world. There have been times of great excitement when you fell in love, got a new job, or moved to a better location. At other times, you faced challenges such as grief, heartbreak, disappointment, job loss, or a health crisis.

Are these cycles on purpose? Is there an order to the way your life and lessons have unfolded? Is there a way to see these changes coming? Is it possible to live in the flow of grace, knowing exactly how to handle every crisis and opportunity?

According to Pythagoras's theory of numbers, the answer is yes!

Every year of your life, says Pythagoras, you've been under the vibrational influence of a particular number—1 through 9 or 11, 22, or 33 within a repeating nine-year cycle. After each nine-year cycle is complete, a new one begins, bringing the benefits and burdens of the last cycle into the new one.

You planned this, of course. You realized you would need many opportunities to evolve your soul and accomplish your mission. You recognized that you would learn certain lessons at certain times in your life when you would be best equipped to make the changes required. You made agreements with your soul mates about when they could enter or exit your life; you created the schedule that would best suit your evolution. You signed up for this timetable and outlined the agenda for your life's turning points!

Let's determine where you are in that nine-year cycle and what is required now to heal yourself from this grief and move forward.

You started this lifetime in the vibration of the path you chose. If your path is the number 5, then the first year of your life was a 5 personal year. The second year of your life was a 6 personal year, and so on.

By adding up your day, month, and year of birth, you'll find your path number as well as the personal year that began your journey. You've repeated those nine-year cycles throughout your life.

Your current personal year is determined by the single- digit numbers of your birth month and birth date added to the current calendar year and reduced to a single digit (or a master soul number of 11, 22, or 33).

Example: Birth date September 15, 1951 Month: September = 9
Date: 15 = 6 (1 + 5)
Current Year: 2012 = 5 (2 + 0 + 1 + 2)
Total: 9 + 6 + 5 = 20 = 2
Personal year = 2

Calculate Your Personal Year
Your birth date:
Your birth month:
The current calendar year: Total:
Reduced to a single digit:
This is your personal year:

Meaning of the Personal Years
Each personal year in the nine-year cycle has its own unique challenges and blessings, successes or setbacks you will learn from and build upon in the following year and throughout your lifetime. Keeping in mind the significance of each particular personal year and how it relates to your soul's mission will help you heal your grief and accomplish your great work.

Personal Year 1
When you're grieving in a 1 year, you feel especially lonely and isolated. But that's because it's a year to focus on *you*—and not on relationships. Your healing happens when you remember who you are, get back in touch with your soul's mission, and own your intuition to move forward on your terms. It's time to launch a completely new and better direction in your life. Start your business, get a new job or title, start a graduate program, or move to a new location. Everything you do this year will influence the events of your life for the next nine years, so you want to take as many positive steps moving forward as possible. If you don't plant seeds for a better future now, nothing will come to bloom as this cycle unfolds. Tap into all the new energy that will help you release your grief and reinvent. There's never been a better time for taking steps forward. Everything revolves around you and is dependent upon you. Believe in your vision, make important decisions alone, and move forward bravely—like a pioneer into your new life.

Personal Year 2
This year, your healing happens when you connect deeply with others and use your wise insights to help them. As you reach out to others in pain, you heal your own grief. But this works only if you've released your past and are not clinging to your losses. Your life won't feel so lonely this year as others step forward to offer support. It's a slower, sweeter year than last year. Success hinges on opening your heart, trusting your heightened intuition, and saying yes to collaboration. It's important to be receptive. Soften the forceful energy of last year. You might feel highly sensitive now, but don't let this get in the way of healing. Your solution is to become the source of love for others, even when you're feeling heartbreak.

Personal Year 11
This is a sacred year for healing your grief. But true healing will come only through your connection to the divine. Your relationships should be focused now on spiritual insights and shared practices of meditation and prayer. It's a year of personal illumination if you use grief as fuel to embrace a new perspective. You'll be inspired to accomplish your most enlightened work. Intuition, inspiration, sensitivity, and artistic creativity are magnified. Make them the cornerstone of your new career. Daily meditation will open a powerful channel of communication with your departed loved one. This intense intuitive connection will provide important guidance. Your spiritual connection is more powerful than ever. Use it as your source for all actions and decisions. Spend time with highly evolved, conscious people who inspire you to create. Small talk and meaningless social engagements will drain you and increase your grief. This is your best year for developing intuitive and artistic gifts as well as healing yourself in a profoundly new way.

Personal Year 3
This is a year to socialize and share your story of loss and recovery. Your grief will ease up when you immerse yourself in the fun, sexy, playful opportunities that come your way. Fully express yourself and create brilliant projects for your new career. Embrace artistic adventures such as painting, music, and dance, and use those outlets to heal. Don't hold back. Get into the center of things, join social groups, and entertain. Forget long-term planning and just enjoy life; don't make important decisions about your future. Develop your skills with words—written and spoken. Whatever you started in your 1 year through hard work and diligence is now reaping enjoyment for you. It's a year to blossom and heal yourself by sharing your creations with others.

Personal Year 4
To heal now, you need to focus on your great work. Just get it done. Next year's energy will push you out into the world to pursue fun and adventure. This is the year to build your house, so to speak. Focus on being responsible and tapping into core strengths. It's a serious year to fulfill obligations, get practical and organized, and build the foundation for your future life. Create your budget and do the physical work. Get

your home in order—whether that means moving, remodeling, or cleaning. Get in shape physically, and cultivate strength in all areas of life. Dependability, honesty, and responsibility are required to heal your grief and move forward.

Personal Year 22

Manifesting inspired work in the world is your key to healing now. Roll your sleeves up and get to work creating new ideas that inspire others. Ignoring your work will leave you feeling off- balance, unfocused, and useless. Use inspiration as your fuel to get it all done. Don't waste time going on long vacations. (You won't be able to relax.) Focus on your great work and trust that fun and relaxation will come later. This is a year for putting personal concerns aside and doing your best for the world at large. Make big plans and introduce changes. You'll have the opportunity to ascend to your greatest career achievements now. Focus on your work and keep moving forward.

Personal Year 5

Healing arrives now in the form of vacations, travel, and adventure. Step out of your comfort zone. Your charisma is amped up and your magnetism is attracting opportunities and people to change your life. Say yes! Be open, fearless, and passionate. Your heart will heal when you expand instead of contract. You'll have unexpected events that turn your life in a new and positive direction. Everything is changing around you. Investigate new career opportunities and get rid of anything or anyone stuck in the past. Eliminate conditions that hold you back. Make room for the new. Focus on freedom and adapting to change. Heal yourself with good food, new relationships, and trips to exotic places—all of which will soothe your grief.

Personal Year 6

This year is a time to heal by offering love and nurturing to others. Embrace family and friends. Open your heart. Become a hospice volunteer or a grief coach. Rather than focus on yourself, focus on the needs of others. Close friendships will blossom as you nurture them with your openhearted energy. Reach out and try to understand the people in your life in a deep way. Let go of superficiality and take responsibility for others. Yet don't take on more than you can carry, or you'll be overwhelmed. This is one year, though, when general harmony and giving love to others are the only solution to your pain.

Personal Year 33

You'll heal best this year when you focus on mystical knowledge, intuition, and spiritual guidance. But if you're not grounded, you could become disconnected to everyday reality. Stay away from alcohol and drugs, and meditate every day. If you embrace your higher self, this will be your most enlightened year. You'll use your intuition to connect easily to your departed. Your pipeline to the divine is opened wide and flowing freely. Take a meditation retreat and connect with your loved ones on the other side.

Personal Year 7

This year, true healing appears only when you take the inner journey. It's time for deep reflection, intuitive development, and spiritual growth. Take meditation classes and spend a weekend in prayer and silence. Strength comes from your connection to the divine. You may feel a bit lonely or isolated. Use your alone time to write a book, research higher consciousness, or take a psychology class. Focus on finding your true purpose. Withdraw from the center of things; social events won't even feel good. Your sensitivity and intuition are heightened; you'll feel other people's feelings everywhere you go. Rely on your inner guidance for all decisions. Don't grasp for what you want— you'll naturally attract what is meant to be in your life.

Personal Year 8

Even if you're grieving this year, money and career will still be your main focus and the topic of nearly every conversation. Pursuing your true work and creating financial success will be the antidote to your grief. You'll have many opportunities to make money and become entrepreneurial, and that should be your focus. It's a year to go to the bank—not the bar—no matter how much your heart hurts. Own your power spiritually, emotionally, financially, and physically. Get back into shape financially and physically. Take command of your own life.

Think big, manage and direct others, and move forward. Be patient and generous to others—and your pain will heal.

Personal Year 9

This year, the answer to your pain is to open your hands and let it all go. Surrendering what you know is required. You'll heal only when you release the past. Friends and lovers from the previous nine years will resurface to be examined, then kept or discarded for the next cycle. Your career and life will conclude the focus that it has had for the past nine years, even though you won't see a new cycle just yet. Have faith that something new and better will arrive next year. You may be fired or laid off, and you'll grieve for your many losses over many lifetimes. Peace comes from higher wisdom and a greater connection to your spirituality. Your insight and wisdom will be heightened. Use this enlightened new perspective to benefit the people around you. Focus on spiritual discipline, and wait for the new inspiration that begins soon in your 1 year.

Saturn Returns

At the **ages of 28 and 29,** you go through your **First Saturn Return.** This is a major transition point of the lifetime—your first true wake-up moment of recognizing your journey for this lifetime and what it's really about. You'll see that your life is going to turn out differently from how you thought it would be. And you'll understand that you're not here to meet the expectations of family and friends. This is your moment of seeing who you really are. You may lose someone you love at this transition point, whether it's a parent, friend, or spouse. This loss is meant to fuel your reinvention.

At the **ages of 58 and 59,** you go through your **Second Saturn Return.** This is the second major transition point of your lifetime—where you're stripped naked until you finally become your true self in the world. You're no longer allowed to hide behind limiting job titles or relationships. It's time to be the authentic self you came here to be—doing your great work in the world. This is also a time when you may lose someone you love and use grief to fuel your reinvention.

Map Your Reinvention Cycles

One of the most helpful steps of your recovery process is looking through all your previous nine-year cycles and discussing what was going on during each cycle. Starting with your birth year, write each year of your life to the left of the personal year number you were experiencing. Also include your age. Make notes by the years when important events occurred—especially note when relationships and careers began or ended, and when you experienced grief and loss. Note any changes that took place when one nine-year cycle ended and a new one began. Note what you learned about yourself during the Saturn Return. By examining your past reinvention cycles, what insights do you have about your current grief challenge and moving through it? What insights have you gained from reviewing your cycles?

Ask yourself the following questions:

How did this cycle begin and end?
What was my intention at the beginning of this cycle? What did I let go of at end of the cycle?
When did I fall in love?
When did I have children or long to have children? When did my loved one die?
What did I learn?
What did I learn during the Saturn Return?
When I look at my Saturn Returns, what can I learn about the purpose of pain and how it fuels my life and great work?

Chapter Nine

Use Your Pain (Anger, Guilt, and Blame) as Fuel

Consider the possibility that all your pain—every wound you've ever experienced, from loss to illness to disappointment—was exactly what you needed and chose to arrive at this point in your life, which is exactly where you're supposed to be.

Imagine that your soul chose to experience this loss to open your heart and strengthen your connection to the divine—to push you onto your true path and inspire you to accomplish your soul's greatest mission.

Cristina's Story

I'm working with a client, a powerful Leo 11-path named Cristina, who lost her mom when she was twenty years old. I can feel and see her mom standing to my right, sending me the message that "all agreements were fulfilled," and that she knows her daughter "loved her very much."

I give this message to my client and she bursts into tears. As we talk, I learn that Cristina had just had a fight with her mom the morning of her mom's death. That afternoon her mom went to take a nap and died in her sleep. The doctors were mystified as to how or why she died in her sleep.

For ten years, Cristina has tortured herself by believing that she precipitated her mom's sudden death. Even though Cristina is now a certified psychotherapist and has a spiritual belief system, she still carries tremendous guilt about her mom. "I was such a brat back then, and so mean to my mom. I wish she could see me now and see the person I've become. I hope she can forgive me."

To my right, I hear Cristina's mom loud and strong in my ear: "I *do* see who you are! I always saw who you were. My job was to launch you on your path as a master soul and healer. All agreements were fulfilled."

I share this message with her. Cristina is comforted but also frustrated that she never hears directly from her departed mother nor can she feel her presence.

Cristina's mom tells me that Cristina's guilt surrounds her with a gray energy that makes it nearly impossible to reach her. I explain this to Cristina and tell her that when she clears away the guilt, she'll hear her mother's voice.

I ask Cristina to do a short meditation with me. We close our eyes and repeat a sacred mantra together until Cristina settles down and I can feel a sense of peace within her. I ask Cristina to speak to her mom. "Tell her directly what you want to say. She's with us now."

Cristina says: "Mom, I'm so sorry I was immature and mean when you knew me. Your death forced me to find my spiritual path and a career helping others as a psychotherapist. Do you see me now? Are you proud of me? Can you forgive me?"

I tell Cristina to close her eyes and hear her mother speaking to her directly. Cristina closes her eyes and listens. Soon she's crying again. "She told me she sees me and loves me," she says through her tears. "I heard her say it."

"When you meditate each morning," I explain to her, "quiet your mind with mantra. When you feel calm and peaceful—speak directly to your mom. She'll answer you. You've cleared the guilt and opened the door for her presence."

Months later, I hear from Cristina. She says that in her daily meditations she feels her mother's love and forgiveness, and that this experience has been very healing. She says it also has encouraged her to trust her intuition in other areas of life— especially when she works with clients. "I'm able to help my clients from a much richer, deeper perspective now. It's very powerful."

Allies for Reinvention: Anger, Blame, and Guilt

Anger, blame, and guilt are natural responses to what's happened to you; they can become your greatest fuel for moving forward. The painful emotions you're feeling today are on purpose. Emotion is energy! And you *need* energy to heal, reconnect to your departed loved one, and reinvent your life!

Whatever you feel, from pain to joy, can be used to help you move forward and accomplish your soul's mission. Feel the anger and use it to fuel your reinvention. It's okay to feel blame at the doctors, at your departed loved one, or at your friends. Harness the power of these painful emotions to fuel your new life and speak your truth.

Embrace the guilt that says you did something wrong that caused the death of your loved one. If you're truly that powerful, what other more positive things can you create now in your life and in the world?

When my husband died, I found myself angry at a God who would let good people suffer. I demanded to know the meaning of life and the purpose of pain. My anger fueled a spiritual and emotional reinvention that eventually brought me here to help you. Now, more than thirty years later, I can shine the light of understanding on the pain of your grief to help you find your way through it. It's why I'm still here.

The Power of Anger: Your Fuel for Recovery or Your Reason for Giving Up

At first, the loss of a loved one leaves you feeling stunned— wiped clean of thought and feeling. In time, the soul-searing pain of grief seeps in.

Because you're a powerful, wise old soul who chose this lesson, we already know you're strong enough to overcome the challenge. We know you wouldn't have preprogrammed this karmic event into your soul map unless you possessed the wisdom to master it.

Because of your enormous strength, you may feel anger at your loss—because anger is more powerful than sadness or depression. If you use this anger to fuel reinvention, it will move you forward quickly.

Realize that there will be many days when you're just plain angry at the world; angry at the doctor who didn't properly diagnose an illness, at yourself for not keeping him home that night, or at God (or the universe) for allowing this to happen. There are countless reasons to feel angry at the loss of a loved one.

When you begin to accept that your departed left this earth according to his own soul contract—not by the action of an almighty being in the sky or a drunk driver on the road—you'll see that you've been left behind on purpose. You haven't yet fulfilled your soul mission. This new and healing idea is the answer to the question, "Why did this happen?" It's the beginning of your soul's awakening. Yet the full ramifications of it will take time to blossom inside you. In the meantime, anger may color your daily life.

Don't waste time asking, "Why am I so angry?" Just feel it and redirect it. Anger *will* get you out of bed in the morning. It carries more energy than depression and will push you out into the world to ask questions, gather information, and get things done. Use anger to redesign your life and create work that prevents others from having to feel the pain you feel today. (To heal your heart, be sure to practice the Break Your Heart Wide Open Meditation first thing each morning.)

Keep in mind that if you hold on to the anger too long, it will eventually shut your heart to the compassion and wisdom you're meant to learn from this loss. Say, "I'm grateful to feel the passion of anger, and I will use that energy to reinvent my career and look for a new spiritual perspective that answers my painful questions. There are truths about how this universe works that lie outside conventional beliefs, and I will find them."

The world will tell you that you're a victim. You won't have to arrive at this conclusion by yourself. You've lost someone you love dearly. This is defined as a tragedy by our left-brain- dominated culture, which doesn't really understand death. Our world isn't quite ready to embrace the idea that our departed loved ones choose to depart for reasons only clear to themselves and perfect for their soul's evolution.

You had a soul agreement with your loved one to stay here and learn who you really are, and embrace a more enlightened perspective on your life. Your departed is your greatest teacher and still tries to offer guidance and love. If you can't feel their presence, it's only because your pain blocks them out.

Grief opens the heart and reveals your true mission. Yet you must dig deep beyond your pain to discover these things; they aren't commonly understood. It's time to go on the inner journey. It's time to let Divine Mother Grief reveal to you everything she came into your life to teach.

There's no church big enough to embrace your pain or help you find your wisdom. You won't find true comfort in conventional ideas. Your healing comes as you shift your perception from this tragedy to a new and bigger idea. This spiritual (but not religious) journey will ease your anger, heal your depression, reveal your mission, and show you why you're still here. It begins with one baby step.

That first step toward embracing this bigger view is daily meditation or prayer. A strong spiritual practice quiets your victim mind, eases your anger, and reverses self-doubt. It opens you up to your higher self, inner wisdom, and connection to your departed. It reveals the vastness of this grand universe and illuminates the truth of the loss you're experiencing.

In your morning meditation, ask your departed how he or she can help you use your anger for reinvention. Ask if he can help lift the burden of pain from your heart and help you see the gift in your loss.

Throughout your day, notice if and when you respond to others with anger. Notice how it makes them feel. Send gratitude, compassion, and forgiveness to those you may have hurt with your anger. And forgive yourself for being angry.

Step out of your comfort zone and visit a different alternative church or spiritual center every week. Try Unity, Science of the Mind, and Buddhist and Hindu ashrams. Discover which of their techniques resonate most with you. Find your new posse of spiritually aware friends and discuss the painful questions of life until you find answers that feel true.

Use this death as an ending to a chapter in your own life. Rename yourself. Go back to school. Start a business. Look for the renewal that comes from death—the rebirth that follows the fire. Embrace this new and healed vision of yourself.

When you fight the flow of your painful feelings, struggle with the natural wisdom of your heart—grief will suck the life from you and take your breath away.

When you learn to trust your grief, relax in it, and allow it to pull you forward in its current—you'll be brought to the shore of your inner wisdom. You'll pull yourself out of the water and emerge reborn. Your departed loved one will be cheering you on.

Using the Clarity of Blame
When a loved one dies, we can easily find someone to blame, whether it's our loved one for not taking better care of herself, the doctors for not

finding an illness sooner, or the drunk driver on the road. Feeling this blame without using it to find forgiveness is like drinking poison and expecting the other person to die.

Powerful blame carries the possibility for powerful forgiveness; when you finally realize there's no one to blame, not even yourself, it opens you up to a more enlightened perspective.

So who *is* to blame for this tragedy? Why did this happen? Why did your loved one leave you? How could something this terrible happen if there's no one to blame? Of course, you want to understand why. You needed them and they left you. Why?

Or maybe they didn't leave you. . . .

Once you grasp the concept of divine order and study your own past reinventions, you'll begin to find your answer. You'll open to the idea that perhaps you chose this grief to fuel your life, to accomplish your great work, and fulfill your soul's mission. You'll consider the possibility that this painful event was part of a larger agreement you made with your departed.

Someday you may thank your departed for fulfilling their end of the bargain. You'll understand that your loved one chose to depart exactly at the perfect moment in exactly the perfect way to fulfill an agreement made before this lifetime began.

When you've spent a day viewing this world through the lens of divine order—where every misstep is on purpose, every death is a brief separation, and every challenge exactly what you ordered up—you're able to move forward and fulfill your soul's mission. It becomes the only thing you long to do.

So . . .

The *only* answer to the question "why?" is because you both chose it. This realization clears your soul of blame and anger and fuels your mission. It opens your heart to embrace true forgiveness and a more spiritual perspective on life.

Embracing the Fire of Guilt

If you're feeling devastating guilt about your loss, it simply means you're beginning to realize how powerful you are. Now it's time to use that power for good.

When a person dies, there's always someone left behind who blames themselves for the death, no matter how ridiculous that may be. Even if your loved one died of cancer, you will most likely tell yourself that you should have gotten her to the doctor sooner, or tried a certain treatment, or found a different healer. None of this is true. When you feel guilty, you're simply misunderstanding the soul mate agreement that put your loss and ensuing reinvention into motion.

Let me assure you that guilt is simply human nature looking for a cause and effect for the things we don't understand. A soul exits in exactly the way and time that they chose to exit. You were simply a player in a preprogrammed drama. You participated exactly the way you agreed to—before this life began. Your loved one left because he was finished with this lifetime, plain and simple. In your pain, this may be beyond comprehension. It requires a larger view possible only through the lens of divine order.

Life is so much deeper and richer than we imagine. We make layers of soul agreements before we drop into this dense realm. You could *not* have prevented your loved one's death, no matter what you're telling yourself right now. It was all much bigger than you. You may not fully understand the plan until the end of your lifetime, when you cross over and review your choices and actions in the light of divine perspective.

If you let guilt keep you from moving forward to do your great work, you're missing the point of this painful event. And you're disappointing your departed, who tries to show you to a higher perspective. The antidote to your guilt is to become a loving, compassionate healer who makes a difference in everyone's life, including your own.

Energy Shifters: Moving Out of Anger, Blame, and Guilt

After you've cried, grieved, raged and blamed and you feel the heavy burden of grief lessening, it's time to begin moving forward and make your departed proud. The first step is to shift your emotions away from the pain in order to have the energy you need for recovery. You're in control of this energy shift and it's simpler than it sounds. Practice the following energy shifters and your life will change for the better. You'll also be raising your energetic vibration which allows your departed to comfort you and connect with you.

Open Your Heart: Love Recklessly!

Your soul chose this pain to help you learn compassion. When you reach out to others in pain, you heal yourself. Focusing on the needs of others now shifts your energy from despair to joy. It's time to become an alchemist and turn your grief to love. Then use the high-frequency energy of love to move yourself forward.

Go back to school and study for a meaningful career that helps others. Or visit your local homeless shelter, family emergency assistance shelter, hospice, school, or church and ask the person in charge how you can help. Go online and search for volunteer opportunities. Pick the volunteer work that most closely resonates with you, your loss, and your gifts. Once you find your gift in volunteer work, turn that work into your career. If you find that you're an awesome listener, become a therapist or a coach.

If you already work at a job you love, show up each day with something inexpensive but heartfelt for a coworker—as simple as a favorite coffee drink or a dried flower wreath you made yourself. Become the bearer of beautiful gifts in your workplace. Offer the love and healing to the world that you're longing to receive for yourself. You'll be amazed at how this heals your heart.

Bring beauty to your grieving family and friends: a scented candle, bouquet of daisies, basket of scented soaps, rose petals in a sachet, or a beautifully framed photo of the one you grieve for. Fill your home and office with roses. Give a rose to someone new each day—for no reason.

In your morning meditation, take a deep breath and send love to one special person you want to wrap in light. Feel it until you can see them in your mind smiling and feeling better. Then send that same loving energy out to everyone around you—and finally to the entire world. Wrap the world in your heartfelt love, and hold that image of the world smiling for as long as you can.

When you meet someone who is being difficult, show them love and compassion. When someone hurts you, respond with forgiveness rather than anger. Doing so will heal *your* heart and release *your* grief. It will lift the cloud of gray energy surrounding you and carry you into the light.

Beautiful surroundings accelerate healing. Spend as much time in nature as possible. Take long walks. Learn to make dried flower wreaths; take a pottery or painting class. Spend your quiet evening hours creating works of beauty and giving them to friends and family for no reason. Fill your living and working space with flowers, color, and light.

Refocus Your Thoughts
Question: What would my loved one want me to do now? Answer: Focus on the future and fulfill your soul's mission.

When our loved ones cross over and complete their life review, they're able to see clearly the great potential we all carry inside— even if they didn't see this while alive. Now they want to help you fulfill your soul's mission and step into your greatness.

You're still here because you haven't yet fulfilled this mission. As soon as you fulfill it by doing your great work, you'll be allowed to be with your loved one.

During your morning meditation, ask your departed what you should do with your life now. Ask specifically for career guidance.

The answer to your pain is "do your great work." But it must be the great work you signed up for, and not menial work done simply to pay the bills. For an in-depth look at this topic, read my first book, *I See Your Dream Job*.

Throughout your day, whenever you feel sad, pick up an inspirational book and see what page it falls open to. Read that page and contemplate how those ideas can help you move forward. Read more of it before going to sleep. Avoid television that depletes your energy, especially when you're feeling down. If you do watch TV, choose shows that uplift you with laughter and inspiration. Fill your bedtime hours with peaceful, transcendent music. Falling to sleep with a good book and uplifting music will put you into a dream state that may precipitate a healing visitation from your departed.

Tell a New Story
To move forward with your life, you need a new story. And sometimes you need new friends to help you release the old story.

If your current friends aren't helping you move forward, join a new community of people doing something you haven't tried before. Take a class in tai chi, hiking, or biking, or join a drumming circle. Enroll in a graduate program that excites you. Introduce yourself as someone going through a personal reinvention, but don't share your specific story of grief. Start new. Let new acquaintances hold you in their thoughts as a happy soul with a meaningful life.

When you spend time with old friends, do new and exciting things with them. Take hikes, visit exotic places, climb mountains. Discuss your departed only in stories that inspire shared laughter and happy memories.

Shift from Superficial to Super-spiritual
When you're having a bad day, focus within: Close your eyes and pray or meditate. Remove your thoughts from the details of our mundane world. By simply repeating a sacred mantra or prayer, you'll soon shift into the higher perspective that eases your pain. There you'll find your wisdom.

Some people turn to drugs or alcohol to try to shift their perspective to a higher state of consciousness. But in the long run, drugs and alcohol only damage your energy and harm your body. These substances knock us off center and make our journey slower and more painful. Using substances to alter consciousness makes it nearly impossible to accomplish what we came here to do.

Begin each morning with the Break Your Heart Wide Open Meditation. This will immediately make you feel better and set a positive tone for your day. You can also do this meditation at work in a quiet space for twenty minutes. Announce to coworkers that you're using your break time to sit in meditation. Eventually, when they see this is real and that it helps you feel better, you'll become a beacon of inspiration. Soon others will be asking if you can help them, and if you'll teach them to meditate. Say yes! You'll be on your way to using your grief to fuel your great work.

Laugh Like There's No Tomorrow
Laughter is a powerful antidote to grief. When we laugh, we raise our energy and embrace the bigger picture of our shared human experience. Laughter connects us and heals our pain.

Find friends who make you laugh, and spend time with them. Bring the laughter into your home. Throw open the windows and laugh out loud at nothing. You'll feel your energy shift to a higher frequency, and you'll notice that your home feels sweeter.

Collect comedy DVDs that make you laugh, and watch them when you're having a bad day. Invite friends and neighbors over for an evening of watching funny movies and sharing popcorn. No dinner required. Simply supply the popcorn and laughter. You'll feel terrific at the end of the night.

Look for the simple humor in everyday events, and share that humorous perspective with others. Making others laugh will fill your spirit with joy. Ask coworkers or family members to share the funniest thing that happened to them that day. Make that your final conversation before bedtime.

Take a laughter yoga class, and learn to release all emotions through laughter. Then share what you learn with others.

Forgive with Abandon!

When you shower forgiveness on everyone, you soon learn that offering forgiveness heals your own heart. When you forgive someone, you're not condoning bad behavior or mistakes. You're simply seeing a bigger picture of our shared human journey. And you're purging yourself of a poisonous energy that will eat away at your soul and damage your own life. You're accepting that divine order is always in action, even when we can't see it.

Healing yourself requires a shift of perspective, from blame to forgiveness. This includes forgiving everyone from the doctor who misdiagnosed your loved one to the friend who said the wrong thing. Climb out of the small-you view and into the divine-order-of-the-universe view.

From this higher vantage point, you'll see your journey more clearly. You'll recognize that you signed up for a big mission this lifetime and wanted to help raise consciousness here. You wanted to get it right so that when you finally crossed over, you'd be proud of yourself, and you'd make your departed proud.

From this divine perch in the higher realms, take an eagle's eye perspective on your life. Observe your soul struggling through its challenges, finding its great gifts, and sloshing through the mud to take the next step. Send big love to yourself and say: "I forgive you, (your name goes here), for trying so hard to get it right and sometimes getting lost. I'm wrapping you in love and forgiveness to help you move forward."

From this wise perch in the higher realms, also observe the person you're angry with. Review their childhood, and see their pain, limitations, and gifts. Give them a nod of acknowledgment. Say, "I know you're doing the best you can at this point in your evolution. It serves me to help you evolve. I can do that by wrapping you in love and forgiveness. My positive energy will help you shift away from darkness." Send them a powerful dose of forgiveness and see their energy shift.

Take a breath and feel wild forgiveness for everyone in your life. Can you feel your pain soften? Practice this until there's no more need to. The weight of blame will have lifted. You'll feel lighter. You'll find yourself owning your greatness, and you'll make your departed proud.

If you're feeling angry at your loved one for leaving you, say to them: "I see that you did your best and loved me as best you could, and that it was all on purpose. I love and release you to your highest good and to your soul's evolution. I trust I will be taken care of and loved here. I don't want to hold you back from where you need to go."

Get Wildly Grateful
Feel gratitude that your loved one was in your life—even for a brief time. Gratitude is one of your most powerful allies in healing. Gratitude is the opposite of sadness, anger, and blame. You can't possibly feel depressed and grateful at the same time. It's like drinking a triple shot of espresso! Gratitude opens your heart and puts you in a high-frequency zone.

Even if it feels like you had only a short time with your loved one before he departed, this is an illusion! You've traveled many lifetimes holding his hand. This lifetime was only a short blip in your shared journey. You agreed to this painful separation to evolve your souls.

When you hear the little voice inside your head say, "Why my husband?" or "Why my child?" just say: "I'm so grateful that I had one day, one month, one year, with my loved one in this lifetime. The love and wisdom I've gained from that experience have enriched me and fueled my reinvention. I'll see her again soon, and when I do, she'll be proud of how I lived the rest of my life."

Sweeten Up!

Grief is sour. It puts us into a negative energetic space that prevents healing and prevents our loved ones from communicating with us. The bitterness of grief can poison you and derail your life. It will keep love away because love is repelled by bitterness. It will keep career success away because success is attracted to positive energy. And it ruins your health by lowering your immune system and draining your chi. Your departed loved ones are saddened to see you feeling bitter. It disappoints them and keeps them from getting close.

How do you shift away from bitterness? By choosing to embrace your divine sweet authentic self. Sweetness is your natural state. You came here on purpose as an open sweet soul on an intentional journey. As you aged, you learned to protect yourself and covered up your authentic nature—because it made you feel vulnerable. But this only hurt you in the long run.

Your sweet self is on purpose and is needed to accomplish your soul's mission. It's also needed to connect with the higher realms. Don't let pain hide your authentic self. When you open up and share this sweet energy with others, it changes your life and heals relationships.

Children live in the energy of sweetness, which they've carried over from the divine realms. Spend as much time as possible around young children. Take them for ice cream, to movies, or to see a play. Children naturally sense our pain and soothe us with laughter and positive energy. By comforting a child, you heal yourself.

Volunteer in a church, classroom, or homeless shelter, and focus on talking to the children. This effort can change your life and give you a reason to get out of bed in the morning.

Spending time with pets also shifts our energy away from bitterness. Being with pets can lower blood pressure, ease pain, and help us heal physically and emotionally. If you have a pet, give the animal extra love and attention because your pet senses your pain and wants to help you. If you don't have a pet, volunteer at an animal shelter. Being in the presence of animals will soothe your soul.

Even in a big city, you can find little pieces of nature where you can listen to the birds or watch children play. This will revive your connection to divinity. Find a park with a peaceful garden. Sit in quiet meditation there, breathing in the strong life force of nature.

Move Your Chi

When a loved one dies, we feel like we've been kicked in the stomach. And we *have* been wounded. Our energy has been depleted by emotional trauma. In my case, when my husband died, I could barely keep food down.

Eventually, you'll discover that you need to move your body to feel better. Rather than waiting for your body to feel better so you can exercise, your body will feel better only when you get up and move around. This is because your chi, or life force, has been depleted.

Even just going for a fifteen-minute walk circulates your life force and promotes healing. It hardly matters what you do—just move! You can walk, run, dance, or jump up and down in your living room. Whenever you do this, you'll feel better in your body and spirit.

When my husband died, he told his best friend, Bill (a world-class mountaineer), that he wanted his ashes scattered in the highest lake in North America. Bill knew that the highest lake was outside of Breckenridge, Colorado—just above thirteen thousand feet of altitude.

Within days of my husband's death, when I was barely able to stand or eat, our friend Bill organized a trek for us to carry Paul's ashes to this pristine lake.

It was a daunting trek, and I didn't want to go. But I had to fulfill Paul's last wish. So I strapped on my backpack and started the arduous journey up a steep canyon to find the lake and scatter Paul's ashes.

On the first night, after hours of exhausting uphill hiking, I saw the genius in Paul's request. As we camped under the bright stars of a Colorado summer night, our bodies trembling with exhaustion, I ate everything given to me and began to feel my chi coming alive. I cried at the beauty of the night sky and felt Paul's joyful presence all around us.

The next day was more arduous. We had to climb a steeply terrifying loose rock wall to reach the glacier-fed lake that rested at the foot of snowcapped mountains. I felt certain I couldn't make it. But we all did.

As we came over the lip of that overhanging rock wall, we found ourselves standing in the most beautiful field of blooming wildflowers I've ever seen. A babbling brook ran past our feet to thunder down the steep wall behind us. It was a sacred space, and it took our breaths away. We held hands in silent prayer and thanked Paul for bringing us there. That day we scattered his ashes into the crystal-clear lake. It was a profoundly emotional ceremony that felt so completely right. By the time we returned home, my body was feeling stronger and my appetite had returned. Paul's final request had saved my life.

Feed Your Chi

Just as when you're recovering from illness, healing grief requires careful attention to the food you put into your body. To heal your soul, you need to heal physically as well.

When you first experience loss, eat abundant amounts of fresh organic vegetables and fruits. Start each day with these energizing foods to cleanse your energy and revitalize your chi. Raw unprocessed food contains life force, and you need plenty of life force now.

When my husband died, I could eat only green grapes for days. People brought me other foods, but they made me nauseated. I stuck with the grapes until I felt better.

It's important to stay away from refined or processed foods— which carry no life force and can deplete your energy. Sugar robs the body of B vitamins, and you need B vitamins for emotional health. Taking a

B-vitamin supplement will ease depression. You'll notice a difference in your mood almost immediately. Eating sugar will give you a temporary rush of energy followed by a huge emotional crash. Sugar feeds depression.

Drink plenty of mineral or filtered water. Washing the negative energy out of your body requires pure water, and lots of it. Putting fresh lemons in your water will benefit both your body and spirit. Lemons provide vitamins and minerals, and they're also used to help cleanse the body and spirit of toxins.

Herbs such as Saint-John's-wort have been shown to ease depression. Visit your local natural foods store and ask the supplement manager for herbs to ease grief. Flower essences such as beech and homeopathic remedies such as ignatia can also help heal grief. These are certainly worth a try before taking pharmaceutical drugs—whose side effects may not be as tolerable to you as those of natural remedies.

Paint your bedroom yellow! Colors have healing power, and yellow has been shown to lift spirits. Wear brightly colored clothing rather than dark colors. They'll have a subtly uplifting effect on your mood.

Avoid alcohol and drugs. You may think you're easing your pain by having a glass of wine with dinner. But you're actually damaging your energy field and clouding your connection to the higher realms. You want this channel to the divine to be wide open in order to receive guidance from your higher self and from your departed. Alcohol and drugs also deplete your body of B vitamins.

See Your Future! (It's Waiting for You . . .)
Once you realize that you're still here on purpose to accomplish your soul's mission, you'll begin to dream of a new future. You'll understand that your loved one wants you to move forward and be happy. Imagining positive possibilities for the future—from love to financial abundance—will reenergize your spirit and heal your heart.

Throughout your day, while driving in your car or waiting for a friend, imagine that you have $5 million in your bank but can use that money only to reinvent your career and find your true work. What would you do with the money? Start a business? Write a book? Take classes or get certified in something you love? Write down whatever ideas pop into your head. This is what you're meant to do now, even without the millions of dollars in your bank account. As you take a few steps forward, exploring this new possibility, you'll put your life into the flow of divine order and find your true work. The money will appear once you've started in the right direction.

See it! Even if it feels a million miles away from where you are now. Feel it, see this new life, and let it make you giggle. Once you're seeing and feeling it, you've called in the highest energy to help you move forward.

Using Grief to Uplift the World...
A great example of using grief to help others comes from the story of John Lennon and Paul McCartney. Their shared grief over the losses of their mothers helped inspire the greatest loves songs of our time. In 2009 I was blessed to visit John Lennon's childhood home in Liverpool. This story is a tribute to his gift of turning his pain into music – music that changed my life.

I'm standing in John Lennon's childhood bedroom at 251 Menlove Avenue in Liverpool, England, admiring its sloped ceiling, small twin bed, and lovely window looking out over the street. This is where John lived and created music for 18 years. Posters of his favorite 60s actress Brigitte Bardot line the wall above his bed, and John's own art sketches and writings adorn his other walls.

From this tiny room was born music that changed the world – especially my world. Yet it's such a small cocoon – this room that fits only me and one other adult – the custodian hired by Yoko Ono to protect the home she refurbished to look exactly as it looked when John lived here until

1963. Yoko donated this home to the National Trust so that it would be forever preserved as part of history.

Colin Hall, the well-educated, soft-spoken custodian tells me that John spent many hours a day sitting on this bed dreaming up a better life – sketching his visions and writing music while he gazed out of this window at the tree tops – all the way to Strawberry Fields – an orphanage a few miles away.

It makes me cry to imagine how John's powerful dream for a better life reached across the Atlantic Ocean in 1964 to touch me – a lonely, young girl growing up in Alabama – and how his dream traveled around the globe awakening so many other people. I remember the moment I first heard a Beatles song and how deeply it rocked my world.

Standing in this room, I can imagine the birth of that powerful music and the pain that inspired John's genius. Closing my eyes, I feel John's creative brilliance burning up these walls, his restlessness, and his dark and powerful grief for the mother he loved who abandoned him – the pain that fueled his work.

"This room brings many people to tears," says Colin standing beside me. And yes, you can feel the sadness that hung over this bedroom when John was brought to live here in his Aunt Mimi's house at the age of five – abandoned by both parents.

By then, John's father had long disappeared. And his mother, Julia, had gone to live with her new boyfriend. Young John was brought to this house to be raised properly by his mother's sister, Mimi, and her husband George. John's mother continued to visit him here and tried to maintain a relationship with John. But she soon started a new family with her boyfriend, and John was never brought to live with them.

In this house, John's new life unfolded. He grew to love Mimi's husband George who became a nurturing father figure to him. But when John turned 15, Uncle George died suddenly - leaving Aunt Mimi broke and desperate for income so that she and John could stay in the house. Mimi took in student boarders – as many as five at a time - to help pay the rent for this two-bedroom house. And John, once again, felt the devastating loss of someone he loved and needed.

It was in this abandoned, struggling world that John spent his hours sketching, writing poetry, playing guitar and writing music. He excelled in art class at his local high school, but flunked his other subjects -which caused endless arguments with Aunt Mimi.

Mimi was convinced that John's fascination with rock and roll would ruin his life, and she only allowed him to play guitar on the front porch. This didn't stop John from pursuing his music passion; in High School he started a rock band called Johnny and the Moondogs - which soon became The Quarry Men.

When John turned 17, his mother Julia, on a visit to see him, was hit by a car while crossing the street in front of Aunt Mimi's house. She died instantly. John was, once again, devastated by loss and poured his pain into music.

That same year, John's band was invited to play for a local church feast and after the gig was over, John was introduced to Paul McCartney, a young musician who was also grieving the death of his mother.

Just a few blocks across town, in an even poorer neighborhood and smaller house, 15-year old Paul McCartney had lost his mother, Mary, to breast cancer. She had been a loving presence in Paul's life and was well-respected in the community as a nurse and midwife.

Her death had devastated Paul, his father, and brother Michael. The McCartneys comforted themselves with memories and music; Paul taught himself to play guitar and write music in the living room of his cramped home in this poorer section of Liverpool.

When John invited Paul to become part of his band, the Lennon-McCartney genius was born. Even though they were young high school boys, they quickly began writing music together – hanging out in the front porch of Aunt Mimi's house, smoking cigarettes, exchanging lyrics, laughing and dreaming up a better life.

Their inspired music that the world came to love so passionately didn't come from privilege, opportunity, brilliant teachers and all the advantages of life today. Instead, their music came from dreams that were launched in loneliness and shared grief.

From grief, came their longing to uplift and inspire others who needed love, who felt lonely, or abandoned. This passionate music that spoke of love reached across the universe - to millions of people longing for connection.

When Beatle music first began filtering into my local Alabama radio station and filling the airwaves of my world with a new sound, a new dream – I was only 12 years old. Yet it spoke to me in ways that John and Paul, light years away, could never have imagined.

From their brilliant new sound, I understood that life was expansive and carried endless possibility. When I heard their voices in harmony, I realized we were truly all connected, and that anyone from anywhere could have an extraordinary life – even me.

How that inspiration was delivered around the world in simple words such as "She Loves You" - was the miracle of the Beatles. Somehow their pain, dreams, and energy carried hope to anyone who felt alone, confused, or lost.

The Beatles created an intuitive connection between people everywhere that started a shift of consciousness in the early 60s. Their simple heart-felt music changed millions of lives for the better. I was one of those people and the Beatles were truly the miracle of my early life. I'm forever grateful for that.

Now, as I turn to leave John's small room and follow the custodian down the stairs of Aunt Mimi's house, I offer a simple prayer of gratitude to John for turning his pain into music. I tell him that I can't imagine a world without his lyrics. And I can't imagine the course my life would have taken without the Beatles. I blow a kiss into the empty room and say "Thank You John."

How ironic that my husband Paul died only months before John died in 1980 – two of the most influential people in my life exiting within months of each other. And now, today, I get to come full circle and thank the first man whose extraordinary gift changed my life...

If you feel lost, alone, depressed, or hopeless, consider this: That dark, powerful pain is your gift. Dig deep and feel it, then use it as your fuel. Make the world a better place by offering to others what you wish had been offered to you.

Take a moment right now to imagine two teen-aged boys from Liverpool living in poverty, with no opportunities for a better future, and grieving the losses of their mothers.

Picture these boys hanging out on Aunt Mimi's small front porch, playing guitar, laughing, and writing music about love – in spite of the grief and pain in their young lives.

Imagine their pure fearless intention, their innocent joy turning itself into magic, into love, and spreading across the universe – changing everything in its path. That was the gift of the Beatles.

Now, YOU try it.... See if you can imagine taking one small step in a brave new direction – in spite of your grief and losses. That step will be your greatest gift to the world.

Part Four

Helping Others

Chapter 10

Stories of Helping Others

In 1984, a few years after my husband died, I was working as a journalist. My editor asked me to write a piece about the Boulder Hospice and weave in my own story. This is what I wrote. . . .

Gwen is a rock. In the way people have of linking with something in your mind—she is a rock. Not that she is rigid or unyielding, but simply as I watch her walk away from me in hospital corridors I want to run after her and hold on.

Gwen helped my husband die nearly four years ago. We came to her terrified of his cancer but mostly terrified of how we were losing control of our living and of his dying. Gwen got us out of the hospital and home. She taught me to punch long hypodermic needles into his rear, to measure his intake of intravenous fluids and his output of urine and bile. She turned my living room into a hospital, me into a nurse, and put Paul back into control.

Gwen works for the hospice. She is the associate director of nursing and has done this for six years. Though it's been four long years since Gwen taught me to give a heparin push in Paul's TPN line, still when I watch her walk away from me I want to run after her. Still, after all this time.

One evening Gwen and I sit in a hospital hallway and talk. I tell her I'm writing a story about the hospice. Gwen is rugged with dark bushy hair and strong features. Pioneer-woman rugged in the way she looks at you—or through you. She doesn't like to mess around.

Now she looks at me like I'm crazy. "Why do you want to write this?" she asks me. I'm not sure, so I blabber away about being intrigued with the strength people find when someone they love is dying. And her, I say, I want to understand how people like her can do this for a living. How could she help me hold Paul in my arms as he took his last breath and the same afternoon help three kids watch their mother die?

Gwen should have been an Outward Bound survival instructor. Survival instructors like to yell at people when they're stuck two hundred feet up on a rock cliff and say, "So did you think it would be easy?"

Gwen has simply always known that strength was required. "My husband died in a car accident ten years ago. For a while, I quit working for the hospice and worked for a family physician. But it drove me crazy with boredom."

In the middle of a crisis, Gwen seems most alive. When the husband is speaking gibberish and slipping further into a coma, and the wife is crying and the kids sitting tight-lipped and stone- faced, Gwen eases into action. She knows what must be done and she does it. She speaks about death the way some people discuss dieting.

And yet she is vivacious and laughs and laughs over silly things—like a patient calling her Wendy or a chart being misplaced. But in the same breath, she'll turn to you and say, "Your husband won't be leaving the hospital again. You understand that, don't you? He's dying now." Her eyes are soft and she looks like she's ready to hold you if you fall and that anything you say or do is okay with her. It's these moments when you want tie a rope around her waist and hang on.

Now Kaye is looking at Gwen that way. I watch Kaye watching Gwen walk down the hospital corridor and wonder if Kaye wants to run after her too. I don't mention this but I notice that Kaye seems unsteady when she turns her eyes away from Gwen and invites me into her husband's hospital room.

Kaye and I sit in chairs only inches away from each other and whisper back and forth. I have never met this woman before but Gwen has told her that my husband died of cancer, so she ends most of her sentences with, ". . . you know that feeling, don't you?" I try not to look at the tall white bed beside us where her husband lies mostly still, but twitching sometimes, and mumbling words that make no sense.

I keep my eyes on Kaye's face. Her eyes lock me in. They are large and brown with soft laugh lines around the corners. She tells me immediately that if she and Tom couldn't laugh, they would never have been able to cope. She finds little stories to tell me that crack her up. She leans back in her chair holding her belly, and the laugh lines deepen. But these are things that most people would find sad. "Don't repeat these things," she tells me. "People would think we're sick."

Kaye is in her fifties, but there is no weariness about her. She has a kind of charged nervous energy—ready to spring from her chair at any minute. Her eyes are always on the hospital bed, even when she faces me.

"Today he keeps asking for Matt, our son," she tells me. I think for a minute that she might cry, but again the eyes lock into mine and hold there for several seconds. Then she looks across the room at her daughter, Jane.

Jane, who is twenty-one, is sitting in a chair with a magazine on her lap. She is blond and pretty and looks like someone who should be going to barbecues and softball games. But she is sitting very still, watching her father. Her eyes seem very liquid and her mouth is one long tight line. When Jane watches her father and her lips tighten, Kaye watches Jane and moves her hands rhythmically in her lap. No one speaks.

Finally someone speaks. Kaye, Jane, and I all turn to look at Tom in the bed. He is calling. The words seem unintelligible to me but the gibberish is quite clear to Kaye. Kaye is beside him now, leaning down close—her ear beside his lips. "You want Matt? He'll be here later, honey."

Tom is on his back in the bed. A maze of clear plastic tubing runs from various bottles and containers to connect with him somewhere beneath the sheets. His face is round and swollen; his eyes are dreamy and unfocused. His lips are puffy. He looks nothing like the man Kaye describes to me as the man she married twenty-three years ago, who was a truck driver for twenty years.

Tom is going to die soon. His cancer was diagnosed two years ago. He has had eight major surgeries in those two years for a brain tumor, lung tumors, spinal tumors, and on and on. Now he is paralyzed from the neck down.

"He walked away from all the other surgeries, but not this one, not this time," Kaye tells me. "Every time he gets critical, we cry and start to grieve and let him go. And the next day he's better and back and forth. One part of me says let him go, and the other part says as long as he's still breathing, there's hope."

Kaye has taken care of him for two years, but especially since January, when he came home from the last surgery paralyzed. When people tell her they admire her strength and could never do what she is doing, she always answers without hesitation, "Yes, you could. You do whatever you must do. And Tom gives me strength."

This brings back memories. It is June 1980. My living room has been transformed. Where once books were lined neatly along the shelves, now there are boxes of syringes, needles, morphine vials, and plastic IV tubing. Inside my refrigerator where once there were tortillas, yogurt, eggs, salad, and beer, now there are piles of clear plastic bags filled with IV solution and bright yellow bags of liquid food called TPN that has become my husband's baked chicken and mashed potatoes.

My husband, who is thirty-five and only two years ago ran the Las Vegas marathon, now is a mass of bones huddled long and lean on the bed that has become the center of the living room. The bones define his face, as chiseled as a monk who has fasted for years. His gaze is far away and vacant.

He whispers gibberish and immediately I understand that he wants a sip of water and that his canister of bright green bile, pumped from his stomach through a long plastic tube, needs to be emptied. I give him the water and begin to empty the bile. This has become ordinary stuff—the way mothers change diapers. I have no feelings at all as I watch the green liquid disappear down the drain.

My friend Merrin is in the kitchen. She comes periodically and cleans with more ferocity than a brigade of magic maids. My dirty counters become the target for her anger—and mine as well. The house seems lighter, sillier when she is finished with the sponge.

Now she stops with a sponge in one hand and the other dripping suds on the freshly mopped floor and says to me, "I don't see how you do it. I could never do it."

It seems an odd thing to say. I've never questioned not doing it. Is there a question? "Yes, you could, Merrin. You do what you have to do. Paul gives me strength."

Now Merrin turns away to wipe crumbs from the toaster. She feels she has been lied to. It seems the most meaningless, empty answer in the world. How does strength come from a dying person who speaks only in whispers and needs a sip of water, a clean sheet, a pain shot, a bath, to sit up, to turn over, to lie down, to use the bedpan? The wife-mother-father-husband-child learns to jump at a sigh, to understand gibberish, to have a second sense about what is needed. Is it so wonderful to be needed? Is it that simple?

Kaye gives no answers to this. To her it is not a question. I sit in her hospital room and watch her checking tubes, temperatures, lowering the bed, adjusting the pillows, phoning home to check on the kids, whispering to Matt to please come to the hospital soon because Dad is asking for him.

Kaye and I have iced tea in the basement cafeteria. We talk for thirty or forty minutes. She tells me that not many families are given the opportunity to mend fences. She speaks about family tensions and adolescent problems and the years when Jane and her father never spoke to one another. She tells me she is so relieved that they've had the time to make peace with one another—and with God.

I tell Kaye about the time Paul woke me up every fifteen minutes because the tube leaked or he needed a shot or the sheets had to be changed because bile had leaked on them. I tell her how I screamed and cried that night and threw a glass against the wall and told Paul I hated him for being sick. She looks at me like we are blood kin and nods and nods her head.

"Tom knows I've been angry at him," she tells me. "And he's even pushed me sometimes. When he was home, that cow bell he had—he'd ring it every couple of minutes."

She looks at her watch. It's been too long. But I have one more question. "What's been the hardest?"

She is quiet for a while, then she says softly, "My kids." For a second I think she will stop now and decide I've invaded too much. But after a while she looks at me again, "When Matt says—Why my dad?"

Now we've crossed the line. Her eyes fill up and she looks away. Both of us sit very still for several minutes. I suddenly feel that the room is too small and notice that it seems difficult to breathe in here. I can hear Matt's voice—Why my dad? Why my husband? I contemplate running for the door, but I sit still. She waits.

Finally, she continues. "But when I ask Matt if he'd wish this on anyone else, after a while he says, 'No, I couldn't wish it on anybody else. We have our belief in God to give us strength and not everybody has that.'"

I am relieved that she believes in God, that something takes away her pain. I am breathing again and the room seems larger and perhaps I'll have another iced tea. She gets one too and tells me that she gets a lot of support from her Bible study group.

Then she says, "Somebody once told me that my faith in God wasn't great enough or my husband would be healed." She just stares at me for a long time like there is a mutual understanding between us of what garbage this is because my husband has died too. She continues, "What do they think? That people will live to be five hundred years old if their faith is strong enough?" For several seconds we simply stare across the empty table at one another, not knowing what else to say.

In the elevator, Kaye tells me how good it is to talk to someone who understands. I am wishing I didn't understand. Tonight I must go home to my empty apartment and make words out of this.

In the room again, Tom wants water, a pain shot, Matt, a fig bar. I step out of the room and sit in the hallway. There are four hospice rooms at the end of this corridor in Boulder Community Hospital. Gwen has worked hard to get these rooms in the hospital. Until recently, the Boulder Hospice has offered only home care to its patients. These rooms have been needed for a long time.

Sitting here in this corridor is like being in another world. A woman comes out of one room and reports on her husband's swallowing a sip of chocolate ice cream as if he had just won the Boston Marathon. Finding just the right position for his pillow assumes the same importance as nuclear arms negotiations. A seventy-year-old woman comes to her door and asks for a reading light so she can read while her fifty-year-old daughter, who is dying from breast cancer, sleeps.

In this other world, I sit taking notes, watching visitors come and go, picking up *People* magazine, and wondering if I can write this story.

Gwen, my former hospice nurse, is there again. I hold on to her with my eyes. She lets me. She sits down across from me and we talk. She tells me about her new baby, Cara, and what an intense kid she is with large eyes and a piercing stare that sometimes makes people uneasy.

I have no doubts that she is just that way. I imagine what it would be like to have a mother like Gwen. I ask Gwen if she will always be able to do this—to work with the dying. She laughs for a long time over this. "I want to take up fiber weaving," she says. We both laugh now, picturing Gwen spending her days in a quiet studio weaving to soft classical music.

"No, I guess what keeps me doing this is my awe of the way things unfold. Like the other night when I was working here and a man died while I was with him. You feel such awe—that moment is so powerful. I can only take a patient so far and then they do the rest. The power of those things beyond our control is amazing."

I know that moment she is talking about. I remember holding Paul in my arms while he took his last breath. I remember the crazy, almost giddy way I felt the moment his spirit left his body and he was free. It was a feeling I couldn't explain to anyone but it made me smile for weeks, looking rather drugged and vacant. My friends thought I was on Valium. But the feeling came from somewhere else. I can't begin to explain it.

A woman comes out of a hospice room and asks Gwen to come help her turn her husband on his side. Gwen disappears into the room and a new hospice nurse sits down beside me to go over her charts.

At first we don't speak and then after a while she introduces herself. She tells me that when she started nursing she loved to work on the Oncology unit because of the level of involvement with the patient. "We worked with them physically, emotionally, spiritually. It was so much more intense than the other wards. So it was a natural progression to come to work for hospice."

After a while into the conversation she mentions that she has had cancer twice. "This last summer when I lost a kidney, I decided I'd quit working for the hospice because it was too difficult. But a little while ago they called me up and asked if I would take on just one patient. And I did. And I was fine. So I guess I'm healed and ready to give back."

She is smiling so vivaciously while she says this that I feel out of breath—like I've been kicked in the gut. I look down at the *People* magazine on my lap and want to read about the mermaid who starred in *Splash*. But I finally look at her and tell her I admire her for being able to work with dying patients when it must touch on all of her fears of dying. "Exactly," she says. "But it inspires me. I see how much these families pull together to get each other through and I see how much love this brings out in people and that gives me courage. It makes me feel stronger."

Several days pass. I go back to the hospital. Kaye and a hospice nurse are turning Tom on his side, helping him to cough, straightening his bedsheets. I walk in and sit down. Kaye sits beside me. "I'm so glad you came back. I wanted to tell you how much your questions made me think. I thought I was prepared for

Tom's dying but it hit me when I went home that night. For two years, my life has centered on Tom. I've felt needed and busy and knew what to do. When he dies, I'll have to face the world again—by myself. I'll have to think about me again. And that scares me. And the kids too. Even now, they have a daddy, no matter what condition he's in. But when he's gone, it will be different. No matter how you prepare yourself there's going to be that crash."

She tells me about the questions she has now. What is the line, she asks me, of prolonging a life? She says that Tom asked the nurse for a sharp knife to cut away the tubes. This has made Kaye wonder if IV lines could be prolonging his suffering. She wonders if giving him antibiotics for pneumonia was the wrong thing to do. Look at him, she says. He's so tired. When she is just about to cry she looks away.

I tell her about how Paul asked me to give him a morphine overdose because he was ready to die. "Could you do it?" she asks me. I tell her yes—out of love. She stares at me for a long time.

(Note: After a year of terrible suffering, Paul ended up back in the hospital throwing up blood and told me it was time to let him go. I gave Paul the prescribed amount of morphine as often as was legally prescribed. His doctors had counseled me that because Paul was so thin and weak the morphine would quickly build up in his system and kill him. This was the only way to do what Paul had asked. I also took away the IV tubes that were giving him fluids.)

Now Kaye's son, Matt, comes into the room. He's a paramedic ambulance driver and he fiddles with the bottles and tubes that lead to his father. He sits down and he and his mother talk across me about their pet boa constrictor, their hamsters, gerbils, dogs, cats, pet rats, and parakeets. These stories make them both laugh and laugh. They tell me about the time the boa constrictor got caught in the lounge chair and the time the bird landed on the cat's head. We laugh and laugh, and this time when I leave the hospital I am forgetting about the man huddled in the tall white bed and giggling about the boa constrictor.

A couple of days pass, and I call Kaye. She tells me she's made the decision to take away all of Tom's IV tubes. "I did some deep soul searching," she tells me. "There's a lot of security for me in hanging on to him. I know what my days are going to be. I don't have to face the world."

Kaye tells me that her son, Matt, the paramedic, is having a hard time with this decision. "He's in the lifesaving business. He told me that we don't have the right to make that choice for anyone. But I told Matt that his dad made that choice a long time ago. The one thing Tom is not afraid of is dying. He's afraid of pain, but not of dying. And he's in so much pain now. So I told Matt we couldn't keep Tom alive for us. We have to let him go—out of love. I never thought I'd have to make this decision."

The hospice nurse who is in charge of Tom's case is named Heather. Heather spends a lot of time now comforting Kaye. They talk about pain control and how Tom will finally die. And how long it could take. Without the tubes to hydrate and nourish Tom, he quickly worsens.

On Easter Sunday, Tom calls for his tennis shoes, his car keys, his jacket. "I'm ready to leave," he says. That night he has convulsions and slips deeper into a coma.

Monday night, Kaye and I stay up late whispering stories back and forth. She tells me about meeting Tom and how he would come and visit with her folks, waiting for her to come home. But when she would get there, he was so shy that he'd get up and leave without speaking to her. "I knew he was there to see me. He was so dumb," she says. This makes her laugh and shake her head.

"I always knew I'd have to get married fast," she says. "If it was going to happen, it would have to happen fast or I'd talk myself out of it. Tom and I started going out in January. We were married in April."

The next evening, the children come and spend time alone in the room with Tom. Kaye wants to be sure that each child has a chance to say good-bye. He doesn't respond to anyone. His breathing is very labored and hard to listen to.

After only a few minutes with his father, Matt, the paramedic, comes out of the room, angry. "I can't take this. I can't stand to see him struggling for breath. Can't we give him oxygen?"

My friend and hospice nurse Gwen appears. She and Kaye talk to Matt about this. "Yes, we can give him oxygen, but it won't help." Matt knows that. He goes into an empty room and shuts the door. Kaye leans against a wall in the hallway and says, "Finally, Matt is breaking down. I wondered when he'd let it go. He needs to do this."

Another hospice nurse is working that night. She goes into the room with Matt and they talk for a long time about how difficult this is for Matt to watch his father suffer and not be able to help. "I'm used to saving lives," says Matt. "And this is my father, and I can't do anything."

Jane spends time in the room with her father. She comes out after nearly an hour, crying. "He said he loved me, Mom." It's the first response he's given to anyone in days.

By noon the next day, nothing has changed. Kaye is sitting by the bed rubbing his forehead. She looks tired. She whispers to Tom, "It's time to let go, honey. We're ready. You don't have to fight anymore."

She looks at me. "I wish he would quit struggling and give up. He's such a fighter." But the labored breathing continues, without change.

We are both sitting in the room talking one hour later when it does change. He takes fifteen short breaths, then does not breathe for fifteen seconds. Kaye counts the seconds on the large clock on the wall beside the bed. "That was fifteen," she says. "He's going now."

Kaye calls Heather, the hospice nurse, into the room. Heather checks pulses and listens to his breathing. She tells Kaye that it won't be long. Then she goes to find Matt and Jane.

Now he breathes eighteen times and doesn't breathe for twenty seconds. Kaye is watching the clock. As each second without breath passes, the corners of her mouth quiver. She turns to Tom. She rubs his forehead. She doesn't cry.

The next time, he doesn't breathe for twenty-five seconds. Jane and Matt sit beside the bed. For several minutes, the same breathing pattern continues. Matt stands up and says, "He'll fight it to the end, won't he?" and leaves the room. He paces in the hallway. He comes back and sits on the floor at the foot of the bed.

Jane leans over her father. She rubs his chest and shoulders and strokes his hair. Tears drip onto his pillow. No one speaks. Now the breathing is very shallow, barely there. But it is rough and gurgly and hard to listen to. Kaye looks down at the floor.

Then it slows. Then it is no more. The room is still. Heather takes his pulse. "He's gone now, Kaye."

The family holds each other. Kaye wraps her arms around Heather and thanks her. People cry, especially Matt. "It's hard to let him go, Mom."

Kaye holds him in the hallway. "I know, honey, I know. But he's not in pain anymore. It's over."

Chapter 11

FIVE GRIEF-HEALING CONVERSATIONS

If you have a friend or loved one who has lost someone they love, you're being called into action to help. This is on purpose. Both of you will benefit profoundly from the deep sharing and communication that can occur when someone is grieving.

When you're grieving, helping someone else who is grieving benefits you as much as it helps them. Your task is to take them gently through these five conversations outlined in the next few pages. This process will help your grieving friend experience a healing shift in perspective.

If you're a therapist or coach, add these conversations to the work you're already doing. I think you'll find that they help your client tremendously.

And if you have a friend or family member who doesn't know how to deal with *your* loss, send them this book!

Conversation One: Tell Me Your Story—How Did Your Loved One Die?

Open your heart and listen. Grieving people need to share their experience and tell their story. In our culture, we're terribly uncomfortable with death. We feel it's impolite to ask someone the details of how their loved one died or how they feel now.

Yet when you connect your open-heart energy with their loss and listen deeply to their story, you become a healer. Stepping into this role will accelerate your own evolution, heal your grief, and give you insights for your own healing.

A story of painful loss can't be fully released until it has been fully told. Become the sounding board and listen to it all, detail by detail. Eventually, the grieving person needs to surrender this story and change their perspective from "here's my tragic tale" to "here's my life-changing experience." Guiding a grieving person through the Five Conversations outlined here helps them make that life-changing shift.

To initiate your first healing conversation, call or visit the grieving person and, with an open heart, ask how it happened. Ask, "What were the final days like? Were you with her when she took her last breath? What did you experience? Have you felt her presence since she crossed over?"

Once you're able to help them start talking, they'll pour their heart out to you; it's a story longing to be shared in all its painful details.

Every therapist, coach, or healer starts with compassionate questions. People who are grieving need to talk and share their pain. It's essential to healing. You can become the healing catalyst for this exchange.

Here are some examples of questions to get you started:

1. Tell me the story of his death. Was it sudden? How long was he sick?

2. Were you with him at the moment of crossing over?

3. What was that experience like for you?

4. Did you have any premonitions or dreams about this death before it happened?

5. Have you had any visits from him or dreams that he was in since his death?

6. What do you believe in spiritually? An afterlife? Heaven? Get them to talk about this and ask very specific questions about what they believe. Don't just ask what church they go to and leave it at that. You want to know what they truly believe in their heart about an afterlife. (Read more about this in Conversation Two.)

7. Do you feel your loved one fulfilled his life mission or accomplished his great work here?

8. Tell me about his life. What did you love the most about him? What do you miss the most? Ask them to share their best memories.

9. What would he want you to do now to fulfill your mission here?

10. If he were standing here now, what would he say to you?

11. What would he want you to do with your life to move forward?

12. What would you say to him?

13. Talk about your own visits from your departed loved ones.

14. Can I help you set up a little ceremony where we can talk to him and you get to communicate the things you needed to say but didn't?

15. Elaborate on the Spirituality Question (see below). During this discussion, ask if they want to explore some other spiritual points of view, whether those are Buddhist, Hindu, Unity Church, Science of the Mind, quantum physics, books about the afterlife, reincarnation. Tell them you'd be happy to go on this journey of discovery with them.

16. How can I best help you, moving forward?

17. Have you had a hard time with holidays or anniversaries? Can we make a plan for getting through the next ones?

Conversation Two: Asking the Spirituality Question
"Tell me what you believe in. "

This second healing conversation may flow naturally from the first one described above. Or you may find that the person is exhausted after sharing the details of their loved one's death. Then you'll want to wait for another time to have this next discussion. Use your intuition to know when it's time.

When you're ready to begin, say, "Please tell me what you believe in spiritually. Do you follow a religion or do you have a daily spiritual practice of some kind?"

Ask the grieving person to share the details of their spiritual journey with you; how they were raised, what they believe in or don't believe in now, and whether spirituality is a focus of their daily life or not. Ask if they pray or meditate every day, and ask them to describe how they do it.

The purpose of this conversation is to unfold the many complex beliefs a person might have to get to the core of their spiritual beliefs—which may be different from their religion. There's a difference between spirituality and religion. Religion is a set of beliefs and rules governed by a church. If the grieving person is already deeply comforted by her church and does not question its beliefs, that's terrific. Just ask her to explain fully what she believes about where her departed is now. You might be surprised at the answers. If the person cites answers that come from his church but the answers don't seem fully fleshed out, keep asking questions. Ask lovingly if those religious beliefs resonate as true for him.

If they're not fully satisfied with their church's answers, it's time to have an open discussion of the bigger picture of spirituality. When they're in pain, their most pressing questions are, "Why did this loss happen?" and, "Where is my loved one now?" By helping them explore a broader spiritual (not religious) perspective, you can help them find answers that are truly healing.

You'll probably find that those who don't believe in any form of spirituality, or anything beyond what they can see and touch, will be in the most pain. They'll feel that their loved one has simply vanished and that life is meaningless and tragic. Yet this loss is their moment of true spiritual (not religious) awakening. It's calling them to experience firsthand their own divine nature. Their pain will diminish the instant they have an experience of communicating directly to their departed.

Having this spiritual conversation with a grieving person will require that you've already taken your own personal spiritual journey to look beyond the limits of religion and find your spiritual truth. If not, this is a great opportunity for you to do so.

To help the grieving person explore this bigger view of spirituality, offer to go on a spiritual journey with him and spend time at a monastery, ashram, or spiritual center. Invite them to step beyond their comfort zone and visit Hindu and Buddhist ashrams, Unity Churches, Science of the Mind churches, Kabala centers, and whatever else they're willing to try.

Becoming a spiritual explorer will open the mind to new possibilities that can be life-changing for anyone who is lost in despair.

The most essential healing piece that you can provide is to teach them to meditate. By quieting their monkey mind, they'll begin to have a personal daily experience of something greater than the physical world. You can offer to teach this daily reconnection meditation described in Conversation Three.

Suggested books to share include *The Conscious Universe* by Dean Radin; *Science and the Akashic Field* by Ervin László; *After We Die, What Then?* by George Meek; and the movie *What the Bleep Do We Know!?* (2004). You can offer to read and discuss a different book or film each week.

Conversation Three: The Reconnection Ritual—Reconnect Them to Their Departed

This ceremony is a powerful way to introduce your grieving friend (we'll call her Ashley) to a healing experience by helping her communicate directly with her departed. Invite Ashley to do this ritual when she's ready. Explain that it's most helpful when she's feeling incomplete about her loved one's departure and needs answers. It can be done by phone or in person, but schedule it ahead of time. You'll need a quiet place to sit, a candle, incense, and a picture or statue of a divine being—such as Jesus, Buddha, Mary, Lakshmi, or your own guru—to bless the space and protect you from negative energies.

1. Call your grieving friend, Ashley, from the sacred space you've created, or invite her to join you in person. First sit in quiet meditation together. Begin by taking several deep breaths. Then ask her to repeat a mantra with you, such as *Om Namah Shivaya* or a prayer such as the Lord's Prayer. Reciting these sacred sounds will connect you both to the highest realms and protect you. After repeating mantra for about ten minutes, when you feel the energy shift and your mind has settled down, go to the next step.

2. Repeat the departed one's full name three times. Ask him to join you in the room. Say: "Please, John, come into the room to help heal Ashley."

3. Tell Ashley to open her heart and fill the space with the love and gratitude she feels for her departed. You should also do this. By filling the room with love for him, you call in his spirit, and you protect yourselves from dark entities.

4. When you feel an energy shift that signals the presence of someone from the other realms, say: "Thank you for joining us. We're grateful you're here, and we're grateful for the chance to heal Ashley. Ashley needs to release you to the highest realms and move forward with her life. Please assist us with this for Ashley's highest good."

5.   Ask Ashley to focus only on the love and gratitude she feels. Tell her to share three happy memories (out loud) that she experienced with her loved one. Then ask her to say three things (out loud) about her loved one that she's most grateful for from their time together.

6.   Now invite her to ask her departed any questions that she needs answers to.

7.   If Ashley crumbles into sadness or rage, let her express those feelings for a few minutes. Then gently bring her focus back to the three things she's most grateful for about her time with the departed. Remind Ashley that her sadness and pain block communication with the departed.

8.   After Ashley asks her questions to the departed, sit together in silence for several minutes. Ask Ashley to write down any thoughts or ideas that pop into her head during this silence.

9.   Close by thanking the departed for his help and asking him to wrap Ashley in healing light to help her recover and move forward.

10. Repeat the mantra or the Lord's Prayer together for several minutes to clear the space.

11. If the grieving person says she did not experience any communication from her departed, explain that the left- brain logical mind was probably filtering out what she received. Explain that doing daily meditation at home will help her learn to quiet her thoughts and open up to her right-brain intuitive perceptions. Ask her to repeat this exercise at home on a regular basis until she's able to receive the messages.

Hook Them Up: Teach the Grieving Person to Feel the Connection
After you take Ashley through this reconnection ritual, it's essential to teach her how to do this on her own at home. We can all learn to access our connection to the higher realms. But it does require the discipline of daily mediation to quiet the monkey mind and tap into our higher consciousness.

Offer to sit with Ashley now and guide her through a simple ten-minute meditation using mantra (sacred sound) or repetition of the Lord's Prayer. Tell her that she can meditate without trying to connect with her departed. Simple daily meditation will open her channel to the divine.

If she's ready to learn the entire process of meditating to quiet the mind and then connecting to her departed, share this process:

Tell her to close her eyes and sit comfortably without leaning her head back on anything. Just as you did during the reconnection ritual, repeat the mantra or prayer out loud together.

After the rhythm of the mantra is established out loud, sit together, silently repeating the mantra for ten minutes. Explain to Ashley that when she notices her thoughts getting in the way, she should gently bring her focus back to the mantra.

At the end of ten minutes, tell her to stop repeating the mantra and open her eyes. In this quiet space, ask her to speak directly to her departed—reminding her to begin with feelings of love and gratitude to call in his spirit.

Have her write down any images, ideas, or whispers that come to her during this process. Tell her she can do this every morning by herself to get daily guidance from her departed. Remind her how essential it is that she learn to quiet her thoughts through meditation to receive messages from beyond.

Conversation Four: Energy Shifters
Healing grief requires a shift of energy from sorrow and sadness to love and gratitude. This shift of energy to a higher frequency is necessary for moving forward, and you can be the facilitator for such a shift.

In chapter 9 of this book, we discussed many ways to shift energy from sadness, anger, blame, and guilt to love, gratitude, and forgiveness. As you talk to your grieving friend, use those potent energy shifters.

Share a funny memory from your life and ask the grieving person, Ashley, to share a funny memory she has of her departed. Share this laughter authentically and observe her energy shift to a higher frequency. Ask her how she can bring more laughter into her daily life as a way to ease the pain. Explain that it makes her departed very happy to see her laughing again. Ask her to tell you three ways she might do more of this, from watching funny movies to spending time with friends.

Use your sweet authentic self to connect with her authentic self. This happens when we share our vulnerability, love, and pain. By sharing your authenticity, you help her open her heart and shift her energy. When we're grieving, we shut the heart to avoid pain. But it's only when we open the heart and feel the pain that we can release it and heal. Teach her the Break Your Heart Wide Open Meditation and practice it with her.

Ask her to tell you one thing that she's grateful to have in her life now. Just focusing on that one thing will help her shift her energy to a higher frequency and allow healing to happen. Ask her to start each day by saying out loud something she's grateful for, and then repeat it again before bedtime. Remind her to be thankful for whatever time she did have with her departed. Gratitude is a potent energy shifter that will make her feel better instantly.

Finally ask, "What would your loved one say to you right now?" She may instantly smile or perk up and tell you that he would say to stop crying or be strong. This is always an energy shift for the better.

Conversation Five: Reveal the Soul's Mission

Grief requires reinvention. Even if Ashley had a powerful career and an impressive education, this heartbreak is her wake-up call to reinvent and step more fully into her soul's mission.

Remind her that she has a witness to her life now: a departed loved one at her side, cheering her on. The departed aren't concerned with our little mistakes, only in seeing that we step fully into our greatness here on earth. If our departed weren't able to accomplish their own mission in their lifetime, they're even more fully invested in seeing that we succeed.

When you feel that Ashley has shifted her energy out of the deep despair of grief by going through the previous conversations, it's time to help her see her soul's mission. It may be a while before she's ready to explore this. You'll know when the time is right by trusting your intuition.

In part 3 of this book, we explored how to calculate your birth path from your birth date and what the path reveals. Ask Ashley for her birth date and explain that you want to explore how her birth date might reveal her purpose here and help her move forward.

Conducting the Soul Mission Session

Schedule a time on the phone or in person. Calculate her birth path, following the steps in part 3. Study the section in this book that describes her birth path and her personal reinvention cycles. Make notes to share with her.

Before you begin the session with Ashley, do a special meditation to access divine guidance for her. Place your hand on the paper where you've written her name and birth path. Then do a twenty-minute, mantra-based meditation. When your mind has settled down, say, "Please, divine guides, give me the wisdom to help Ashley move forward."

When the session begins, start by asking Ashley to sit in quiet prayer or meditation with you for two minutes. During this quiet time, ask again for divine guidance to help this soul move forward.

Begin by sharing the meaning of her birth path as described in chapter 7. You can read her the entire section about her birth path. Ask if it resonates with her.

Bring your own authentic sweetness, gratitude, and humor into this conversation to help Ashley relax and open up to the information. Ask open-ended questions such as, "How does that feel to you?" Or say, "Share with me any ideas that pop into your head as we read about your path." Write down the ideas she shares.

Explain the meaning of the personal reinvention cycles as described in chapter 8. Point out where she is now in her nine- year cycle, and read the description of that personal year. Ask if that description gives her ideas for moving forward. Spend some time reviewing all her nine-year reinvention cycles and what changes occurred at each reinvention point. Help her see how change and reinvention have always been a part of life.

You'll know if this conversation is helping her when she begins to share ideas about tweaking her career or finding a new kind of work. Remember to use the energy shifters of gratitude, humor, and sweetness if she feels overwhelmed.

Create a Baby-Step Action Plan

It's important to list action steps for each idea you discuss. For example, if she says she wants to take a psychology class, make a list of Web sites for her to visit to find the right class. Action steps can include daily meditation, books to read, people to meet, and spiritual centers to visit.

Repeat these action steps clearly at the end of the conversation to summarize them for her. Be sure to give her the written list. Remind her that if she feels overwhelmed to focus just on the baby steps. End the conversation by asking, "How else can I help you with this information? How else can I help you move forward?"

Chapter 12

FOUR STEPS TO HELP LOVED ONES CROSS OVER

For six months, my father had terrible back pain that no one could diagnose. Doctors poked, prodded, and scanned, and found nothing. "You're just depressed," said my brothers. "You need to exercise," said the doctor.

I lived miles away in Colorado, yet from weekly phone calls, I knew there was something more going on. I *knew* he was dying. On the phone one Sunday, I asked, "So Dad, do you think you're dying?"

"Yes, I do," was his heartbreaking, honest answer. I made plans to fly home.

Seventeen years earlier, my husband, Paul, had died and I had relied heavily on my dad's love since then, often saying, "You can't ever die, Dad. I need you here with me." And he was always there for me. I knew that if it was his time to go now, I had to release him. So I sat down and wrote a letter.

In a heartfelt letter, I told him how much I loved him, what a great dad he was, and that I would be okay if he needed to go now. I said I would love him forever and we'd always be connected and would find each other in the other realms. It was the hardest letter I ever wrote.

On the day he received it, my brother told me that he read the letter and left the office for the day. I can only imagine he was coming to terms with his own death—even though no one, especially the doctors, agreed that anything was wrong with him.

I hadn't seen my dad for six months, and when I arrived home, I knew instantly. He was gaunt and tired; I'd seen that look before. We sat in the sunroom and talked. He cried to me in whispers, not wanting to upset my mom. "It's okay, Dad. Everyone will be okay. . . ." I tried to comfort him as he had always comforted me.

The next day, doctors performed a new test and found a tumor hidden behind his heart. They gave him a few weeks to live. I spent the first night after that diagnosis sitting with him in the hospital bed, reminiscing. He didn't want to talk about the cancer, the treatments, or the family—he just wanted to remember his New Orleans childhood. I was a willing partner for the process.

In the morning, after spending the entire night holding hands, listening to his memories, regrets, and unfinished dreams, he told me that our talk had meant everything to him and that now he was at peace.

This was how the evening unfolded as we sat in the hospital bed, holding hands and watching his favorite TV rerun of *The Cosby Show*:

"I was so lucky," he said softly above the din of audience laughter coming from the TV. "I really had a great childhood."

"You did," I whispered. "Your family was wonderful—brilliant and funny . . . it doesn't get better than that."

My dad closed his eyes to remember: "We knew everybody in Algiers. There was always a gang of kids to play with. People spent their evenings on their front porches talking to each other. They'd say, 'Hey, Tommy! Tell your mother hello!' Or they'd tell me I should get home for dinner."

He continued: "Did I tell you how we took the ferry across the river every morning to go to school? There'd be a taxi waiting on the other side. Sometimes we'd squeeze ten kids into that taxi. . . ."

We both laughed, and then my dad was silent for a while as *The Cosby Show* continued. Finally he spoke again: "One summer when I was a kid, my father came home with train tickets for the whole family. He told us to each pack one small bag of clothes. The next day we got on the train and spent three months traveling the country. I'll never forget it.

"And Long Beach," he continued. "Long Beach was heaven." Now his eyes tear up and neither of us says anything.

Long Beach, Mississippi, was my family's nirvana. It's where my great-grandfather bought coastal property and built two identical family homes separated by an oyster shell driveway. A huge water oak with low-hanging mossy branches stood at the entrance to the drive, a babbling creek ran behind the property, a sugar cane field grew next door, and a white sandy beach stretched in front of us as far as we could see.

The warm Gulf water was shallow and calm, perfect for long afternoons fishing and swimming. We could walk half a mile out before the water got deep, and there were freshwater springs that bubbled up impossibly from the sandbars at low tide. We drank straight from those springs nearly every day, pressing our cheeks hard against the sand to sip the freezing water. It was like a dream, impossible and yet real—until 1969.

Hurricane Camille took it all away, leaving only two concrete slabs where our homes had once stood. Dish towels hung from the tallest trees—remnants of sacred ground that had once housed our entire extended family every summer. My grandfather had a stroke and died shortly after. My grandmother developed dementia. My dad never got over it. I left for college soon afterwards and never returned. Hurricane Camille scattered our family in every direction.

"I'm so sorry, Dad," I say. "I wish it had never happened."

There's a long silence while we watch TV and then he says: "You know I really wanted to be a jazz pianist in the French Quarter. That's what I really wanted to do with my life—either that or become a priest." We both laugh.

"Why did you become an engineer?" I ask.

"Everybody wanted to be an engineer back then. I worked on ship engines during the war. I never looked back."

"You're the best dad in the world," I whisper. "We had a great childhood because of you."

"When I think of all the golf games I was going to play and all the fishing trips I was going to take . . ." He grows quiet. Occasionally he shares another memory and we talk about it.

As the sun begins to rise outside our window, Dad asks me what I believe in spiritually. He raised us Catholic, but he knows that I've since pursued other spiritual paths and that I meditate every day.

I gently try to share my view of the divine realms, reincarnation, soul mate agreements, karma, and the ongoing journey of our souls' evolution. He listens intently. "I know you're very spiritual and that you're a good person, but it worries me that you're no longer Catholic. I know where I'm going when I die, and I want you to be there too."

"We'll find each other, Dad. I promise."

He explains that he wants to talk to the priest the next day and confess his sins. He wants me to do the same so that I'll be with him in heaven eventually. I agree to do this, knowing that it will give him peace and help him let go.

Eventually he dozes in and out of a restless sleep.

In the morning, they take him downstairs for a medical procedure, and he never fully recovers except for brief conversations with family members and with the priest. He's gone in three weeks.

As a child, I had the gift of clairvoyance. When I woke up screaming in the night, unable to fully bring myself back into this realm, my dad would walk with me, holding me on his shoulders, pointing to the nursery rhyme characters on the wall to bring me back here and calm my fears. When I was older and still having those nighttime episodes, my father would have me sit beside him to watch Johnny Carson until my world came back into focus and I was no longer stuck between the realms.

Now, I become his guide to the other realms—helping him release his past and slip through the thin veil between the worlds.

The Four Steps
Sharing final moments with dying loved ones, I've discovered a powerful process for helping people cross over peacefully. You can follow the four steps below to help your loved one at the end of life. This four-step process moves them through the necessary stages to be able to let go and fearlessly cross into the divine realms. These steps have helped everyone I've shared them with—no matter what religion or nonreligion they practiced.

Step 1: Open the Door
Asking a loved one, "How do you feel about dying? Do you think you're dying now?" may seem like a terrifying or intrusive question to ask. Yet the most helpful and empowering thing you can do is discuss death honestly with your loved one. They're longing to discuss their feelings and fears about crossing over; their soul knows it's almost time to go. When everyone else is in denial and afraid to directly broach this topic, it's your job to start the conversation. The dying person will be so grateful to have someone they can speak to honestly.

Ask your loved one how they feel about dying. Discuss it in depth. Ask: Do you think it's your time to die? What does dying mean to you? What are you afraid of? Is there anything you feel needs closure?

Listen carefully. The answers tell you how to proceed. If your loved one has fear of dying or isn't confident about their own spiritual perspective, you're meant to be their spiritual exploration companion. Find out if there was a religious belief in the household when they grew up. Were they involved in a church? Was it meaningful to them or did they outgrow it? Have they explored any other spiritual paths since walking away from the one they grew up with? Is there a path they'd like to know more about now—whether it's Buddhism, Catholicism, or metaphysics? If so, bring them information about those beliefs or share your own observations about those paths.

If they're very logically based and don't believe in anything they can't see or touch, discuss what the quantum physicists teach— that we're all composed of energy, pulsing light that can never be destroyed or diminished. Share your own personal experiences of spirituality (but not religion) and what they mean to you.

Invite them to pray or meditate with you to feel the presence of something greater than the physical world. Teach them this meditation if they're open to it:

Sit beside them with closed eyes. Take several deep breaths. Teach them how to repeat a sacred mantra such as *Om Namah Shivaya* or a prayer such as the Lord's Prayer.

Explain how repeating this for twenty minutes will quiet their fear and help them tap into their higher self. It will also help connect them to the loved ones waiting in the other realms to guide them. At the end of twenty minutes, say: "Please help me feel my divinity and embrace the guides who are here to help me cross over peacefully."

Step 2: Clean House

The dying person is longing to review their life story. Memories are flooding back as they finish up this final phase of the lifetime. Invite them to share these memories with you. Ask direct questions about their childhood and early life. Listen deeply.

This life review process begins naturally inside all of us when we face death. Sometimes family members don't want to review these memories, because they aren't ready to let the dying person go. Yet reviewing the past is essential for a peaceful death. You can be the brave one who facilitates this healing process for your dying loved one. They'll be forever grateful.

If you're afraid of death, your fear will prevent the dying person from being able to fully open up and process their experience with you. This is a good opportunity for you to deeply explore spirituality and embrace a bigger view. You're being asked to evolve your own soul to a higher level of consciousness by going through this process with your loved one. This is part of the soul mate agreement you made long ago.

First, you will need to do your own inner work. Meditate and clear your consciousness of the fears and attachments that you carry for your loved one. Sitting in silent meditation while repeating a mantra for twenty minutes will begin to quiet these fears and open you up to your higher consciousness. After doing your own inner work, sit with your loved one and begin the life review conversation.

This is a time for forgiveness, compassion, and honesty that will serve you and your loved one.

Questions to get you started include the following:

1. Ask them to relate a favorite memory from growing up. Ask for details of the memory to help them focus on it.

2. Share your own favorite memories from their life.

3. Point out the things they did well or the people they helped.

4. Share what you're grateful for about them being in your life.

5. Ask: How do you feel about dying? Do you think you're dying?

6. Ask: Do you feel ready? Why or why not? What are you afraid of? What are you waiting for?

7. Ask: What do you believe happens when you die?

8. Ask: How can I help you explore the dying process and prepare for it?

9. Explain the process of death as the spirit gracefully leaving the body with a final peaceful breath. Explain that they'll immediately feel free from the burden of the body. Share any stories you have of seeing the departed on the other side.

10. Tell them they're in charge of the death process, and they don't have to struggle and suffer. They can choose to go to sleep and leave their bodies peacefully when it's time. Tell them to visualize making their exit clean and peaceful—merging into the divine light of God.

11. Say to them: I love you so much and will always miss you, but I'm willing to let you go if this is your time. I'm not afraid of where you're going. I know you'll be in a realm that's as close to me as the clothes I'm wearing are to my skin. I'll feel you with me every day. I'll be fine, I promise.

12. Ask: Is there anything you need in order to feel peaceful about dying? Is there anything that needs completion? If they've been estranged from someone, this is the time to make the phone call to forgive that person. Or invite that person to come visit. Or they may be waiting for a loved one to arrive from far away. You can help with all of this.

13. Do your own inner work. Forgiveness and surrender are required from you. Your loved one is attached energetically to you. When you're able to go deep inside through prayer and meditation to release them, you help them let go peacefully. This takes powerful inner work on your part. I've included two stories by my friend Katherine to illustrate how she did this with her mother and brother. Her story about her mother's crossing appears below.

Katherine's Story of Helping Her Mom Cross Over

Being a busy person, I was looking forward to doing some inner healing work on my beach vacation with my husband and daughter. Having had powerful results with self-forgiveness meditations and exercises in the past, I gave myself over fully to the process. Being on vacation, and usually so busy with business, brought up the fear of emptiness and a self-loathing for feeling empty and not knowing how to enjoy my time off. So, I began working on the process of forgiving myself for feeling empty and for taking out my fears on others.

The process led me to realize that emptiness being a bad thing was an idea implanted by my mother when I was young. You had to be busy, social, and doing something to feel valuable. I stayed with the writing and meditation, feeling the deep process of forgiveness uncovering a lot of pain, but giving healing air and light to the wound. And then, I had an experience that I have never had before. During the meditation I felt a gray blanket of fear and anger at my mother just lift off me and float away. It was as if it were corporeally real. I felt so clear and loving of my mother, a woman with whom I had not had an easy relationship. It was one of the truly powerful experiences of my life.

The next day the call came. My eighty-five-year-old mom, who had been sick but was still quite vital and strong, was not doing as well as expected. I got on a plane right away and went to her side. She had deteriorated quite a bit and was now in danger, although expected to live. I sat beside her and was able to do so with equanimity, free and clear and able to just be there for her.

After several days by her side, she had recovered enough that I was planning on going home. The day I was going to leave, I went to the hospital to see her. Her doctor stopped me in the hall and gave me the news: Mom's kidneys were failing and she was not expected to live more than two to three days.

I called my siblings, and they all came to the hospital. We spent time with the social workers and many others to make end-of-life decisions. We decided to move her directly into hospice and let her pass as peacefully as possible. Then my sisters and brother went back to their families, and I spent the afternoon sitting quietly beside my mother. I sat with her for four to five hours, holding her hand and meditating on her life and her spirit. Silent tears poured down my face—mostly because I had never seen her spirit so clearly before. I had no baggage, no anger, no need to process my relationship with her. My issues had floated away in that gray blanket of anger, and I could just focus on her and her needs.

My siblings came back that evening and brought my father, whose dementia seemed to vanish as he said good-bye to his wife of fifty years. I cannot describe that moment. It was too precious to put into words. Since my siblings all had kids and families to take care of, and my own family was eight hundred miles away, I volunteered to stay with my mother that night. She was still able to communicate with gestures and a few words. And she said that she was relieved that I would be staying with her.

Again, I sat by her bed and went into a meditative state of letting her spirit go, and releasing all binding, limiting thoughts and feelings. It was quiet and peaceful. The hospice nurses gave me a cot so I could sleep beside her. I woke every thirty minutes or so to check on her. At 2:50, I woke and she was still breathing, slowly but rhythmically. I fell back asleep and awoke at 3:15. She was gone. I sat beside her, held her hand, and felt the freedom of her spirit. Her body was a shell; life had departed.

The gift I was given, of being released from the anger and pain that I had carried for my mother and then being able to be there for her as she passed, has had a powerful impact on my whole life. I feel freed from the issues for which I blamed my mother, and I respect her life and my own more fully.

Step 3: Hand Over the Key
Our souls are completely in charge of the dying process. We pick the exact last breath of the lifetime. We may not be consciously aware of this, but our soul is completely in charge of entering and departing this physical realm.

When someone is afraid of dying, they may have a fear of losing control. This is your opportunity to help them see that they *are* in charge of the process.

Invite them to meditate on a peaceful death with you. Sit beside them and do mantra repetition until your mind has settled down. In the quiet space, say, "Let's see a peaceful exit from the body into the divine light—without struggle or fear." Picture this for them even if they can't do it themselves. Hold the vision for them.

Explain that when the time comes, they don't have to struggle and suffer. Tell them they can go to sleep and leave the body peacefully. Tell them to imagine making this graceful exit without pain or trauma.

Ask if they want prayer, chanting, music, incense, or essential oils to help them ease the transition when it's time to cross over. Ask if they want people to gather around them in prayer, or do they want to be alone? Follow their instructions.

Step 4: Set Them Free
Bring in loved ones and friends who still need to release him. Have each person spend a minute or two alone in the room, sharing what they're grateful for in their relationship with him, what they would like forgiveness for, what they want to forgive the dying person for, and expressing clearly that they'll be okay when he's gone. This is very important, whether or not the dying person is still conscious.

If you realize that you aren't ready for him to leave, you need to do your own inner work to free him energetically. You don't want his death to be a struggle as he waits for you to release him. Meditate at his bedside and open your heart. Say, "I release you with love for your highest good." Visualize him taking a peaceful last breath and leaving his body without fear or struggle. See a departed family member helping him make the transition. The more inner work you can do to release him, the more you empower him to have a graceful death.

When you sense his energy is beginning to let go, sit beside him, rubbing his arms and legs. Tell him that he's free from his body and it's okay to leave now. Tell him to take a final breath and let go. When he's gone, say prayers or sacred chants over his body, instructing him to move to the highest realms and toward the light. Don't plead or beg him to come back. This will hinder him on the other side. Let go.

Katherine's Story of Surrendering Her Brother Frank

My brother Frank was thirty-nine when diagnosed with pancreatic cancer and given a few months to live. I was thirty-four and was working closely with a spiritual teacher who guided me to help him. My teacher told me I had to do what Frank was having to do—let go.

In Frank's case, he was letting go of his health, his vitality, his dreams and desires, and finally his life. At thirty-nine years old, he became like a very wise old man until he passed.

My spiritual teacher was a wise man and did not tell me what I had to let go of. I had to dig deep in myself and find those things that were most binding and limiting in my life and let go of them. I started by giving away prized possessions. I knew physical possessions were just a symbol and that this was just a beginning.

After deep meditation and an inner scanning of my emotional ties and bonds, I realized that what I most needed to truly let go of was my desire for my family's approval. The fourth of five children from two very powerful and successful parents, I had looked for external validation from my family my whole life. This had to die within me.

(Note: The award-winning TV series *Mad Men* is loosely based on the life and work of Katherine's father, who was a creative and brilliant advertising executive in the 1960s.)

The internal struggle that ensued was like an epic battle in my heart and mind. I had to do the internal work, and quickly, or I would not be able to truly help my brother. All I wanted to do was help his soul, as I understand it, be able to release this lifetime peacefully.

I went to my favorite mountain retreat, and there I spent several days crying and battling my internal family demons—placing before my mind's eye all the voices, thoughts, and ways I had lived to please my family. I realized I had lived most of my life with that inner screening process: All my choices and actions first had to go through a mental audition in my mind to see if they would be approved by someone in my family. I was not living an authentic life. I was living my idea of what my family wanted.

This realization was so powerful, devastating, and liberating that I came down from the mountain a different person. It was not the end of the battle, but I knew what I needed to do. I had to live my life from my truth and power, not from some idea of what others wanted.

When I went to see my brother Frank, I never told him what I was doing. I needed to be an example. But in his ethereal state, he gleaned the change in me the moment he saw me, and together we talked about how to let go, how to pass into freedom from the mortal coil, and how to live life fully by dying often. Frank said, "No one is helping me more than you are. You're doing the important work that is making the real difference for me. Live your *life, Katherine."*

I helped Frank pass. I know that as surely as I have ever known anything, but he helped me live.

Part 5

Your Grief Recovery Workbook

Step One: Feel and Release the Pain
It's necessary to feel your pain in order to release it and heal. Daily meditation is a powerful way to do that. Commit to practicing the Break Your Heart Wide Open Meditation in chapter five.

Step Two: Reconnect to Your Departed
The Daily Reconnection Ritual and protection techniques in chapter 4 will reaffirm the eternal and loving bond you share with your departed loved ones. See chapter four to begin using these powerful tools.

Step Three: Your Daily Healing Schedule
By following the Daily Healing Schedule outlined in chapter five, you are dedicating your waking hours to healing the pain of loss and accepting your soul's mission.

Step Four: Calculate Your Birth Path
After calculating your birth path number (found in chapter 7), write a brief summary of your path, including the suggestions for healing grief.

Write your ideas for how you can use this information to realign your life.

Describe your Golden Key and how you might find a new direction by aligning it with your birth path mission.

Step Five: Review Your Reinvention Cycles
Write a brief description of the personal year you're experiencing right now and the implications it has for your healing. You can calculate your personal year by following the formula in chapter eight.

Beginning with the year you were born, review all your past nine- year life cycles; make note of your age, the calendar year, and the personal year cycle you were in for every year of your life. Remember that if you're on a 5 birth path, the first year of your life will be a 5 personal year. Chart your cycles from there, beginning a new nine-year cycle when each one ends.

Study these reinvention points, noticing when you fell in love, experienced heartbreak or loss, started a new job, or lost a job.

Write your thoughts on how understanding where you are in your personal year cycle now can help you heal your grief.

Step Six: Use Pain as Fuel

Write your thoughts about the challenges and lessons you chose for yourself before embarking on this lifetime.

Tell or write the story of your loved one's death. In the story answer these questions:

1. Describe the moment of his crossing over or the moment you learned of his death.

2. What was your immediate response?

3. What insights do you have now about this loss that you wish you had known sooner?

4. What soul lesson was your departed loved one teaching you by putting you through this loss?

5. What would your departed want you to do with your life now?

6. If you knew your departed was here beside you, what would you say to him?

7. From your most spiritual perspective, what has been the gift of this experience?

8. What three steps are you willing to take to bring spiritual purpose into your daily life and work?

9. What steps are you willing to take to use your pain as fuel to accomplish your soul's greatest mission?

Describe how you might shift away from anger, blame, and guilt by trying a new perspective, as described in chapter 9. Write your thoughts, and turn them into an intention statement to help you move forward.

Step Seven: Shift Your Energy (from chapter 9)
Describe how you can bring each of these eleven energy shifters into your daily life:

Open Your Heart: Love Recklessly
Refocus Your Thoughts
Tell a New Story
Shift from Superficial to Super-spiritual
Laugh Like There's No Tomorrow
Forgive with Abandon!
Get Wildly Grateful
Sweeten Up!
Move Your Chi
Feed Your Chi
See Your Future!

Now that you've completed your Grief Recovery Workbook, remember to continue the Daily Healing Schedule and your daily meditations. This process will speed your recovery, bring your life into the light, and help you fulfill your soul's mission. Your departed will be proud of you!

About the Author

Intuitive Sue Frederick's work, described as "a breath of fresh air" and "an enlightened new perspective," has been featured in the *New York Times,* CNN.com, *Real Simple, Complete Woman, Yoga Journal, Fit Yoga,* and *Woman's World.* She's been a guest on more than two hundred radio shows and numerous TV shows, including *Bridging Heaven & Earth.*

Her workshop venues include the New York Learning Annex; Omega Institute for Holistic Studies in Rhinebeck, New York; Naropa University; Loyola University; National Hospice Association; the American Business Women's Association; and the National Career Development Association; Unity of Phoenix, Unity Southwest Conference and Unity of Boulder.

As an intuitive since childhood, Sue draws upon dreams, numerology, and conversations with spirits to help you "see your soul mate." She's the author of *I See Your Soul Mate: An Intuitive's Guide to Finding and Keeping Love* (St. Martin's Press), *I See Your Dream Job: A Career Intuitive Shows You How to Discover What You Were Put on Earth to Do* (St. Martin's Press), and *Dancing at Your Desk: A Metaphysical Guide to Job Happiness.* Sue is an ordained Unity Minister, master numerologist, and spiritual coach.

To learn more about her work and to receive a free bonus e-book, visit www.BridgestoHeaven.com/bonus, e-mail her at Sue@Brilliantwork. com, or visit www.SueFrederick.com

Printed in the USA
CPSIA information can be obtained
at www.ICGtesting.com
CBHW020820300124
3814CB00044B/872